Mom, I'm Telling On You!

A volume of telling tales about one awesome mom!

By V. Kevin Martin

Mom, I'm Telling On You!

Copyright © 1999
V. Kevin Martin

FOR INFORMATION CONTACT:
V. Kevin Martin
Post Office Box 4180
Killeen, TX 76540

ISBN: 0-7392-0455-6

Printed in the United States by:
Morris Publishing
3212 East Highway 30
Kearney, NE 68847
1-800-650-7888

Dedicated to my mother,
who will forever be an inspiration to me.

Although some names have been changed
to protect the innocent and the guilty,
this is for you!

TABLE OF CONTENTS

Tattletales

While I traveled with my evangelizing parents in the early years of childhood, there were so many experiences defying the imagination that Mom refused to write about them, declaring that the book would be classified as fiction and that no one would believe her autobiography.

Most of these outrageous tales seemed to revolve around Mother and her various phobias, ideas, opinions and inspirations. One of those phobias was mice. My mother was deathly afraid of mice. She often claimed that a mouse could literally scare her senseless.

On this particular occasion, it was not Mom who was frightened nearly to death; it was I. After reading this anecdote, you may possibly understand why we were never allowed to keep hamsters as pets. . . .

Chapter One

The Mouse Hunt

How did I live with a six-foot-four mom in a five-foot tall camper? Answer: I slept under the table. Sound crazy? You don't know the half of it! Every night that I laid my head beneath the oversized dinner tray that we called a kitchen table, I said my prayers. These were desperate pleas!

Now I lay me down to sleep.
I pray the table doesn't leak,
And if it falls before I wake,
I pray it holds a chocolate cake.

Those were the kinds of petitions we Martin kids prayed with a fervency seldom heard by more fortunate children—youngsters who lived in a "real" house.

We (meaning myself, my two sisters and my dad) lived in a fifteen foot travel trailer with Mom. Granted, it was a few inches taller than five feet, but it seemed to shrink when Mama stood up. The space diminished remarkably when she was mad, an event we wanted to happen less than once a century.

Mom, I'm Telling On You!

There simply was no room for disharmony. We had to get along! Cleaning house meant standing in one place and scrubbing everything within arms' reach. When a visitor dropped by, someone had to sit on the steps outside to make room for him or her. An umbrella lounged beside the door for the possibility of rainfall.

Mom was a good preacher's wife, doing her duty to support her evangelist husband while raising three kids, teaching youth groups, giving puppet shows and writing stories for the UPCI Sunday School department. She was as busy as a needle in a sewing machine, endeavoring to juggle responsibilities and raise a family at the same time. She tried; she really did. But sometimes, it was too much for her to handle, and she would get fed up.

By fed up, I mean her patience wore thin. I spent much of my childhood learning to recognize the signs that preceded those infamous episodes when Mom went "on a tear" (as in rip, pluck, cleave, shred, slash, sever, . . .).

Oh, I don't mean literally. Or physically. She would never lay a hand on us in anger or frustration. She didn't have to! All she had to do was stand with her head bumping the ceiling of that tiny camper, put her hands on her hips and thunder, "All right. I've had enough." Five seconds later she had all the peace and quiet she wanted. Nobody, but nobody wanted to hang around when Mom went on a tear!

On one of those memorable occasions with Mom complaining about the walls closing in on her (they didn't have very far to go), Dad bought the "Dumpster."

The Dumpster was fully eight feet longer than our old camper, and it sported several major improvements. The ceiling was tall enough so that Mom didn't bump her head, offering some degree of comfort to her. However, not hearing that muted thud gave us kids less time to run when her tolerance fizzled.

The Dumpster was supposed to be a marvel of modern technology. In addition to the extra length and height, this freak was engineered to expand to roughly twice its original width. The two halves fit together like a Velveeta box on its side, and a hydraulic system performed the ritual of its opening and closing. At one location, the hydraulic function failed. The church we were "blessing" had three weeks of unplanned revival while Dad and a local mechanic repaired the contraption.

Beauty was not its strong point. It truly looked like a dumpster; we never parked behind Taco Bell or McDonalds for that very reason. We traveled over the southern United States with the monstrosity following us.

The particular locale providing the setting of this drama eludes me. It was somewhere in Arkansas. I do know that we were parked near a meadow that nurtured large, healthy field mice. This story is about one of those creatures unlucky enough to find himself in the Dumpster.

. . . It was midnight. Dark and silent. The smallest sound could be heard. Nothing could sneak past the quietness of a still, summer night such as this. Not even a mouse.

Looking for food in the Dumpster that night, the unfortunate rodent was skittering about the kitchen floor, honing in on a stray bread crumb from the evening meal. It had no way of knowing that in the next few minutes, its presence would alter the life of a young boy forever. Intent on its journey, the small animal continued its exploration. The faint sound of scurrying feet carried around the kitchen wall to the bed where my parents lay sleeping.

"What was that?" Mom sat up in bed and shook Dad awake. "There's something in this trailer!"

Dad, wise man that he is, did not argue. Rising and mumbling to himself, he stepped to the kitchen to find the source of disturbance. I will always believe my life would have been much different if Mom hadn't followed Dad into the kitchen that night.

After several minutes of muttering and searching, Dad decided to open the cabinet door. He lifted some towels to see if the mouse was there. It was. It froze, and so did both of my parents.

Time hung suspended for the merest of seconds. Then, suddenly, the little creature made a mad dash for freedom, trying to escape the horrors of this madhouse. It ran toward Mom.

Mom screamed, an earsplitting cry of dread and despair. Seconds became an eternity as the scream echoed from the walls of the Dumpster. The sound gathered volume, shattering my dreams into a thousand shards of terror. It vibrated, filling my heart with unspeakable horror and fright.

I slept in a bed which folded into a couch during the day. (Almost everything in the Dumpster folded, except money.) The bed was just around the corner from where Mom and Dad were valiantly fighting the monsters. Mom grabbed a broom handle and waved it in the air like a baton, yelling at the top of her lungs.

"Get him!" she screeched. "Kill him! Don't let him get away!" The baton descended with a resounding crack.

"Ow!" Dad yelped from his stance on his hands and knees. The frightened rodent had escaped the broom handle, but Dad wasn't so lucky.

"Here he comes!" Dad bellowed as if describing the demons of Hades. The *thing*, whatever it was, was headed my way.

"Get him, Elroy!" Mom shrieked. "He's coming after me. Get him–oh, there he is! Ohhhhhhhh!" Mom threw the broom and ran.

The wail brought every imaginable monster hiding in the depths of my mind to the surface. Truly the end of time had come, and tribulation would devour me any minute! A petrified cry tore from my lips, fervent and panicked.

"Lord, have mercy! What's going on here?"

Mom's broom finally quit its wild, mid-air gyrations. She sat down with a gasp. Dad closed the cabinet door, and blessed silence reigned once again.

They both looked at me, seeing my hair standing on end, covers held in a death grip, my teeth chattering. Suddenly Mama laughed. It was a small titter, the beginning of mirth.

The convulsions of laughter grew into hysterics. Dad sat beside Mom as they gave way to great, heaving howls, holding their sides in merriment. Long and loud they guffawed, their humor finally ebbing to a low rumble. Then new eruptions broke out.

I became angry. Why were they laughing? It wasn't funny. I was scared out of my wits! Tears rolled down my face.

"Don't laugh; it's *serious*!" I said in a voice as grown up as I could manage.

For the first time they saw just how frightened I was. In unison, they came to my bed. They took one of my hands in each of their own. Then they joined hands. Presently it was not three separate people against the monsters, but it was one family facing their "enemy." I felt the fear vanishing. We prayed together, and after a while, I fell asleep, holding to their hands.

The incident has long since passed, and upon recall it has caused many a chuckle among our brood. But the message was one I will never forget.

I now have a family of my own. To this day, when we face adversity, I gather my wife and children about me. Joining hands, we unite and pray as one. That act of unity breaks the hardest of times into manageable slices.

That childhood incident, however scary at the time, taught me a great lesson: Unity is power. The legendary "mouse hunt" has helped me to escape many, many traps in life.

Tattletales

One of the things that never fails to amaze people about my mother is her sense of what is needed to make everything work together. The dictionary defines this as "intuition." Mom has incredible intuition about life in general, which created many wondrous hours for her offspring as we grew up. However, there were times when her intuition strayed.

When she was right, she was awesomely so, but when she was wrong— Well, you be the judge in the upcoming account. It is true and correct to the best of my remembrance although I could be on the moderate side of this disaster. . . .

Chapter Two

Stars & Strikes Forever!

There are Christmas dramas, Christmas broadcasts, Christmas novellas, and if you have a mom like mine, there are tragedies that would make even Shakespeare weep.

No one was prepared for what happened that night. The hand that appeared above the cardboard stable was the handwriting on the wall for our project.

We, the six of us, sat about four rows back in the dimly lit church, gazing at the stage in front of us. A straw hut, a rock-faced town and a manger, all made of cardboard, carefully constructed and painted, shimmered in the suffused glow of hidden lighting. My best friend sat next to me, looking on. It was the week before Christmas.

Our fingers were sore and our brains numb from work. We had spent hours painting over ink plastered boxes. Nailing. Gluing. Wiring. Caulking and duct taping it all together. Several miles of extension cord provided the electric lighting, and a tired, old stereo threatened to leave the angels without their "harps" at any given moment.

"Well, that does it," I said wearily.

"Did we miss anything?" My friend was a worrier, always thinking calamity was just around the corner. How I wish I had been a little more like him on that occasion!

I looked over the stage again and glanced at the list in my hand. Each line had a tiny, perfect check beside it. My future wife, the coordinator of the group, had meticulously examined each item. All was complete.

"Don't worry," I reassured him. "I don't think anything major *can* go wrong. We have everything in order; now, let's just have fun and enjoy the drama."

He relaxed. In fact, all six of us did. As we perched there in peaceful confidence, a contented grin our faces, we forgot about Mom.

I sat holding the list (which did not include Mom) and thought how smoothly the drama was unfolding. Little did I know that this night would be forever burned into my memory. By burned, I mean literally!

At five-thirty, the cast assembled. Everyone was there except for Brother Mac, the "backstage manager" who was *never* late. I panicked for a moment, thinking of the many people who depended on him for their cues. What should I do? Not to fear, though. The faithful brother arrived a few minutes later, mumbling about a flat tire and apologizing profusely for his tardiness.

After a brief prayer, I asked if anyone had a comment before we headed for the dressing rooms. Dad (the pastor) thanked everyone for his or her efforts and said he believed this drama would impact many lives. (Was he ever right!)

Mom then stood and said she was sure it would be an unforgettable evening. Had I known what she really meant, I would have refrained from my final speech.

"You all know your parts," I assured the actors, "but remember that the audience has never heard them. If you

18

forget, just improvise. If you think it will fit, then do it!" Oh, those treacherous words. Why, oh, why didn't I think about Mama?

The church began filling with people; there were many first-time visitors. We had advertised our drama for two weeks prior to the big night. It was almost time for the play to begin. I donned my Radio Shack headset and checked all the other stations. Everyone responded; they were ready.

"Up music. Tape one. Stage lights." The stage lighted and soft strains of music filled the auditorium. People began snapping pictures. Everyone was excited and waiting. So far, so good!

"Everything looks perfect!" I told the intercom. Oh, the cost of ignorance!

The play ran flawlessly; each did his part. The audience laughed, gasped, clapped and cried at the right times. It was too good to be true!

Then came the final scene, the one with Baby Jesus in the stable outside the inn of Bethlehem. The crowd sat in rapt attention. Even the old record player performed at its best, belting angelic melodies without a single hiccup.

With only a few minutes remaining, my chest swelled. *Mark this one up as a success,* I thought, still forgetting about Mom. A sputtering, crackling sound brought a quick halt to my smug pride. Something was happening backstage.

"What's going on back there?" I asked the backstage manager.

"Huh?" Brother Mac was more than a little hard of hearing. He was, however, very talented with extension cords and hiccuping stereos, thus his position near the stage.

"I said, 'How's everything backstage?'" I repeated slightly louder.

"Okay." Brother Mac was long on loyalty but short on words. I wanted more detail. A bright, dancing light flickered eerily across the church's white ceiling. Something was wrong.

"What is that light back there?" I inquired again, hoping for a few more words this time.

"M'tchz," was the reply.

What . . . ? "I'm sorry, but I didn't hear you," I prodded.

"Matches. Oh, never mind. . . ."

Fear sprang into my mind. What didn't match? Or was it matches? Next to several gallons of paint and cardboard and wood?

"Who has matches?" I yelled into the little, black microphone next to my lips.

"Not that," was the confused reply. "Okay, here goes."

Here goes what? I thought.

I didn't have to wait long.

We were in a small church that would seat a hundred and ten people sitting elbow to elbow. There were no windows. The paneled walls reflected light very well.

As a camera flashed, the stage flared with a bright glow. But the flash was not leaving. Its reflection glowed near the top of a piece of cardboard painted as a rock wall. *Wait a minute! That isn't a flash bulb.* My mind clawed for rhyme and reason as the prospect of a trouble free Christmas production crumbled before my eyes.

A hand appeared above the manger, waving and gyrating. The angels had stopped singing and were now staring in openmouthed shock at the apparition. The hand held a bright ball of fire that shot sparks and smoke from its center.

20

"All right! Who's got a sparkler above the manger?" I hissed, seething. *Who would ever do a crazy thing like that?*

"Huh?"

"I said, 'Who's got a sparkling firework on top of the stage?'" I blurted into the plastic mike again.

"Huh?"

Dear Lord, let him hear me just this once, I prayed. *I'll pay double tithes, I'll*— "Sparkler!" I fairly shouted, thinking that everyone must hear me by now. "Who has a sparkler back there?"

"Sister LaJoyce." *Mom!*

In Texas, they sell fireworks from roadside stands through the Christmas holidays. Somehow my mother had obtained some sparklers, and wishing to make a "real star," she had lit one backstage over Baby Jesus! I turned stricken eyes toward my dad, who had left the audience and was hurrying to my side.

The angels attempted to find their cue to start their song, but the old stereo/cassette system had changed songs and was blaring a number from the next scene. Dad reached my side and looked at me inquisitively.

"Mom," was all I said. He understood.

"How many of those things does she have?" he asked as another "star" appeared, its comet-like core spitting smoke and light. I had spots in my eyes from the intense glare.

"How many of those does she have?" I relayed into the intercom.

"Huh?" Oh, Lord, to have a megaphone . . .

"How many . . . how many sparklers does Mom have?" I enunciated each word carefully.

"Doobozzes," was the reply.

"What?" I demanded.

"Two boxes." Ten sparklers per box. Twenty sparklers. *Oh, merciful . . .*

"Tell her not to light another one," Dad said, using great common sense. Already the small auditorium was filling with smoke. The angels were coughing, and the soldiers were crying albeit not from exultation nor conviction.

"Tell her not to light another one," I echoed into the microphone.

"Light another one, yeah." Before I could punch the talk button again, another sparkler appeared.

"*No! Don't* light another one," I called backstage, now desperate. I was past caring whether or not the audience heard me.

"Huh?" The "huhs" were becoming epidemic.

"Not another one. *Don't— Stop!*" I was frantic. Wood and cardboard burn when fire is present.

"Don't stop, yeah," I heard as two more fire sticks appeared. These were laid on top of the stable which had been freshly coated with flammable paint. The smoke increased in density.

The old stereo sported a single cassette player in its delapidated front. We hadn't the money to buy blank tapes, so we had recorded our drama music onto donated ones. Thus, as a sparkling "star" made of gunpowder cavorted above the smoke-filled manger and the Christmas music ended, another travesty beset us. Someone forgot to turn off the tape player. A man named Oliver Sain and his jazz musicians began to serenade the newborn King with secular lyrics and rhythm.

A soldier offered the angels a handkerchief. A guest on the front row was crying, and the three wise men, using

22

common sense, left in due haste out the side door of the church. Dad sprinted for the stage.

Standing outside the front doors of the church, I shook hands with visitors and friends alike. Many had tears in their eyes, and I wondered if they were touched by the message or were simply feeling the effects of Mom's impromptu "star" above the manger. I got my answer when a portly gentleman stopped to shake my hand.

"You know," he remarked, "I really enjoyed the drama although I never did quite get the sparkler thing." He stopped to cough away some smoke. "Anyway," he concluded, "it was an unforgettable performance."

It was indeed, I thought, smiling, *sparklers and all!*

Tattletales

Hospitality has always been one of Mom's greatest virtues. LaJoyce Martin never meets a stranger. Young and old, rich (which we were not) and poor (which we were), expensively attired (were not) or dressed in homespun hand-me-downs (definitely were), you were welcome at the Martin house. Here homesick Bible school students found solace, as well as lonely soldiers, the homeless, passersby. We had many of them as guests at one time or another.

All this hospitality created quite a strain on Mother's nerves, especially when guests outstayed their welcome—which was often due to her wonderful homemade meals.

Mama seldom complained, and never, ever did the visitors know that they were a burden. But even Ms. Hospitality herself had her limits. The following is a true narrative, written to the best of my memory, of how we, the Martin family, ran away from home. Enjoy!

Chapter Three

Missing!
Family of Four...

That the FBI didn't publish a wanted poster about us is a wonder. I expected any moment to be hauled in, fingerprinted, questioned and put on eternal probation all because of another of Mom's harebrained schemes.

Our family lived in a halfway house, which meant it was too far for visitors to continue to their destination but too close to return where they had been. Mom was too busy to clean house, so she redecorated. I don't know how many times she rearranged, but she never had to dust.

We kids had fourteen or fifteen "unofficial" sisters and brothers, at least six sets of "uncles and aunts," and enough weekend company to start our own congregation. I suspect at least two-thirds of the innumerable host at the marriage supper of the Lamb will be looking for Mom's homemade yeast rolls!

The incident herein recorded comes amidst a period of occupancy that would have made Noah's ark seem spacious.

We had a live-in father and son, as well as a few homesick soldiers underfoot. With Fort Hood only a few miles away, all the homesick soldiers came either to our house or to Rev. William Dean's house (a pastor and friend in Killeen, Texas). A group of Texas Bible College students had just departed after consuming several hundred of Mom's rolls, preaching a few services and staying awake all night playing ping-pong.

The doorbell rang, and Mom opened it to find another hungry family who were "passing through" and thought they would "drop in."

"Dropping in" is a term that means "we have used up all our vacation money, we're tired and hungry, and we need a place for the night." I looked at Dad; he had that deer-in-the-headlights look, both helpless and exasperated at once.

Mom's smile never wavered, but I could see the wheels turning in her head. *Let's see, fifteen extra tacos, eight sheets, four blankets, pillows, towels, more yeast rolls, . . .*

"How *kind* of you to think of us." When Mother emphasized a word, there was usually a different interpretation to be attached. Mom was getting a little weary of so many drop-ins. Regardless, she set about making the new family comfortable, inviting them to stay for supper.

Mother's cooking is world class. Nobody's variation could come near to the excellence of Mom's taco salad (hamburger meat was cheap back then) with bean and cheese nachos and guacamole. Every person at the table ate until he was miserable.

Eventually the subject of where everyone would sleep arose. Mom could not turn anyone away even if there was already a crowd. I'm surprised the city didn't put a bus stop at the end of our sidewalk! On the night of our mysterious disappearance, Mom was in fine form as a hostess.

"Mercy, no! There's no use in y'all going off to some expensive motel and wasting all that money. Y'all just stay here with us tonight!" Mom was heaping up the hospitality. I decided then and there that my room was not going to be clean when Mama went to find beds for everyone. You see, if my room wasn't clean enough, my mother was too embarrassed to let company stay in it, and I got to keep it for myself. I was planning a serious muddle for my room when Mom stopped moving.

Still is not one of Mom's normal behavioral patterns. A person is hard pressed to keep up with her, and if he starts late, he'll never catch her. She invented the term "busy bee."

"I'm sorry, I didn't catch what you said." Mother was in full pause, so I stopped to listen, too.

"I said that we are enjoying this so much, we should just extend our vacation for a few days." This comment came from the father of the family.

"Oh, yes, Daddy! Can we? Can we?" Did I neglect to mention that the kids were four- and six-year-old wrecking machines? Even our scrappy poodle was in hiding. The youngest consistently yelled at the oldest, who was practicing to be the loudest drummer in the world by banging his fork on the table.

"Why— That would be just wonderful!" Mother smiled, but the spark had left. Things were careening out of control. As she scoured a pan for the second time, her head bowed in fierce concentration, I actually felt sorry for her. *It's not fair,* I thought, seeing my mother dive-bombed by a plastic jet. *Mom shouldn't have to go through this.* I was almost willing to clean my room and relinquish it for the night when her head lifted.

Mom, I'm Telling On You!

She looked directly at me and winked.

Her grin was slightly insane, one that told you to get ready for anything. I smiled to reassure her and headed for my room.

Soon the party was in full swing. A concert of laughter and yelling created a bedlam impossible to penetrate with rational thought. I abandoned the frivolity and sought the solitude of my room. But I couldn't banish the noise. It was worse than the sound of a freight train!

Angrily I increased the volume on my radio, trying to drown out the commotion. The din outside my door doubled in intensity as if someone had turned a knob or opened— My door *was* open!

Filling the door frame was my mother. She still had that insane grin on her lips; only now it was wider, more pronounced. Her lips moved, but I couldn't hear her over the clamor.

"What?" I yelled.

She beckoned me to her, bending toward my ear as she spoke. "Pack a bag," she said.

"What?" I asked again, not quite comprehending.

"Pack a bag, a suitcase. Take everything you will need for the next three days. Hurry, but don't let *them* see you." By "them" I inferred she meant the multitude currently pillaging the rest of our house. I looked at her questioningly, but she just smiled that crooked smile and closed the door.

She's gone off her rocker, I thought, but I packed. Placing the suitcase by my closet door, I drifted back into the living room to watch the circus.

Around one o'clock in the morning, the gaiety began to wane. Only a spattering of activity remained. Brief bursts of machine gun fire still exploded from the plastic plane as its pilot refused to land and retire to bed. Whispers and subdued giggles could be heard as the guests began to settle down.

I lay quietly listening to it all. *Why,* I wondered, *did Mom ask me to pack a suitcase?* It was weird; that's what it was. Just plain weird.

Suddenly I sat up in bed, frightened. There was someone at my window! They were . . . yes, they were tapping on it!

"Who's there?" I asked.

"It's me. Mom," came the whispered reply.

"Mom? Is that really you?"

"Shhhh!" she motioned through the window. "Come here."

I opened the window. It was indeed Mom, and Dad was standing beside her. Now he, too, had that wild, senseless grin on his face.

"Get your suitcase. Hurry up, and be very quiet!" Mom commanded.

"But—" I began to question.

"Don't ask questions. Just bring your bag here. Move it!" I moved it, handing my suitcase out the window to Dad. Mom was already at the window of my sisters' room, knocking urgently. Suitcases were shoved out their window.

"What are we doing?" I found the nerve to ask.

"We're running away," Mom stated.

"Running away? From our own house?" So this was Mom's maniacal plan. Running away. Great! "But what about all our stuff?" I was a little skittish about the fast turn of events.

"It will be here when we get back," guaranteed Mom.

"But all my toys . . ." I argued.

"Look," Mom placed her hands on her hips, turning to look me squarely in the eye. "We're getting out of here for a while. If they want the house, they can have it, and if you want to stay with all that crowd, you can." Put that way, running away from home sounded good to me, too.

"But what will our company think?" I asked while heading for our Dodge van.

"They'll figure it out sooner or later." Dad, as usual, was right. Together our family quietly boarded the escape vehicle and drove away into the night.

As soon as we were out of earshot, Mom began yelling, "We did it! We ran away from home!" Soon we were all laughing and having one the most enjoyable times of our lives.

When we came back to our halfway house, several faces had changed. The plastic jet sat mired in the shag carpet of the living room, and our dog was out of hiding. The routine was at its normal, frenzied pace. They had hardly missed us!

"What's for supper?" someone inquired.

"How about hobo stew?" Mama replied. We runaways looked at each other and grinned.

Tattletales

One of our favorite family subjects is music or, rather, Mom's version of it. When LaJoyce Martin and music come together, the result is destined to be both inspirational and unforgettable!

From the earliest years of my childhood, music was a major part of our family. Mother played the accordion and piano. Dad played the guitar or mandolin or trombone. No Christmas was complete without at least one "family jam session."

Grandpoppie Berry played the harmonica. PaPa Martin sawed a mean fiddle while the grandmas sang.

One of my favorite memories is the night Mother chased a piano across a stage platform. That and a few other memories make up this next chapter. . . .

Chapter Four

Mama's
"Big Bang Theory"
(A re-enactment based on faulty memory)

"Let's all turn to page three-fifteen," the song leader intones solemnly. Pages rustle as church members and visitors alike search for the correct page in their hymnals. Someone coughs; a baby cries. The ceiling fans whir with a monotonous hum, and a mischievous teenager giggles at a nearby distraction.

All of this is lost on me. I sit entranced, a small boy alone on the front seat, waiting for the war to start. You see, I always sat on the front bench in revivals. I sat there for two reasons: so Mom could watch me and so I could see the war. It didn't matter where I sat as long as it was by the main instrument. What I mean by main instrument is that Mother played it. I should tell you that any instrument my mother played was the lead instrument whether it was the accordion, piano, organ or bongos.

Mother believes in worshiping with all her body, soul, mind and strength. And where Mom is concerned, that is an awe-inspiring combination!

The audience is waiting now. Some are aware of what is about to transpire, but some are visiting the church for the first time. *Heaven have mercy on us all,* I breathe as the action begins.

Mom raises her hands high above the notes, and the beehive bobbles precariously. Oh, did I tell you about the beehive? It's hard to describe, but I'll try. Mama had several favorite hairdos, most of which could be characterized by using animal or vegetable names. There was the swan-do, a graceful, curling hairdo only eight or nine inches high that took several hours to prepare. Then there was the onion bun. It, too, took a surprisingly long time to fix because she had to remove all the tangles from something she called by another bestial name; I think she called it "ratting" her hair.

When all other hairdos failed, Mama fixed the beehive. It was a "hurry up and fix it so I can get to church on time" hairdo. The beehive was famous around our house because it always preceded the war, the battle between her and the piano.

When Mama got frustrated about her hair, she would storm from her room and bundle us kids in the car. She could not wait to get to church to start the war. But back to my story.

Hands poised in the air, beehive swarming above her concentrated features, Mama paused. One could almost hear the word "Attack!" shouted in her mind. (My dad says that Mom doesn't play the piano; she attacks it.) Believe me, pianos the nation over trembled on beehive night.

When the hands descended, the war was on. Boom, bah, bah. *Boom,* bah, bah, bah. Dum-dum-dum-dum-dum-dum-dum-*dumdumdum, BOOM, bah, bah, bah!* I looked across the congregation to the visitors. They were sitting mesmerized, watching the war progress. As the verse of "Power In The Blood" wound into the chorus, violence is the only way to describe it.

The revival I speak of was taking place in a school in Wesley, Arkansas. The last thing hosted before our service was a dance. I'm sure the piano would have preferred waltzing over war.

As the service accelerated, Mom became more and more anointed. "Power In The Blood" surrendered to "O I Want To See Him" or some other song, pounded out on the old grand at the speed of sound.

Suddenly the music stopped. Right in the middle of the song! I looked, as did everybody else, at Mom. She was bent over on the stool. *Oh, no,* I thought, *the piano finally won the war!* But it was not to be. Mom had her hands underneath the piano and was pulling it back toward her. *Why did she do that?* I wondered.

The music started again, and this time I watched. The piano was moving! On the freshly waxed dance floor, the piano was bouncing, jumping, and with each leap it was trying to escape from Mom and the war!

Mom's beehive had transformed into a UFO (Unpinned Flying Obstacle), and her face nearly disappeared as she opened her mouth in another fortissimo chorus. Why, I wondered, did she have to go through all that commotion? Why couldn't she be normal like other piano players?

It took me years to realize the truth: Mom was not simply playing the piano. She was worshiping with all her might. As I recall those "beehive" nights of war and worship, I remember that when she worshiped, others worshiped. With her total devotion to God, she led them to give their all.

Mom, I'm Telling On You!

To this day, Mom still attacks the piano, and at times she wears the "beehive." I live far from her now and cannot be there on those special nights, but sometimes if I close my eyes and listen closely, I can still hear the thunder of Mom's piano playing. Shouts of praise were lifted as people won battles over many sources of oppression while Mom fought "the war."

Tattletales

Mom and Dad shared their hearts and souls, as well as their time and talents, with many people. Countless lives have been touched by their God-given ministries. Among those who received this blessing were the kids that we called Youth Campers.

A brief note found while scouting information for this book stated that the Martins had just returned from their fifth camp of the year; those five camps included 2010 campers and 15,460 scrambled eggs!

Together, the Martin clan participated in thirty-five camps over a period of fifteen years. The Texas District Campgrounds at Lufkin, Texas, will forever be remembered by my family as a place where we enjoyed some of the best times of our lives.

During the twelve years that our family served in Texas District, happy memories were made, and many poems, songs, skits and dramas were written by LaJoyce Martin. The following chapter is a collection of these memories and includes some of the original and hilarious youth camp songs for which Mom became famous—or infamous.

Chapter Five

Disorder in the Court

She walked in wearing a gigantic, floppy hat decked with plastic flowers. The brim of the straw headgear flapped and wobbled as she took her seat. Her dress (clothing stores are probably still trying to find a name for that garment) also sported flowers, but they didn't match the hat. Nothing matched the gargantuan shoulder bag she hove into the seat next to her. The shoes were somewhere between Brooks Brothers and Ringling Brothers, and the— Oh, never mind; you get the picture!

Mom sat down and smiled her twinkling, impish smile, and the whole room brightened instantly. Everybody was smiling. Sis. LaJoyce Martin had arrived and just in time.

". . . and all staff will be in place by eleven a.m. in order to receive the campers. Are there any questions?" Bro. David Myer from Groves, Texas, as Camp Principal and Coordinator, looked over the assembled group of deans, matrons, cooks, guards, teachers and office staff, waiting for a raised hand. The pause lasted about a millisecond.

"Yes," someone called, "we'd like to hear Sis. Martin sing, please." Everyone clapped and yelled encouragement. Bro. Myer's lips parted in a smile of surrender. It seemed a youth camp couldn't begin without one of LaJoyce Martin's famous songs. (The songs were always slated at the end of the staff meetings because there was no way to restore order after one of those ignoble renditions!)

Mom's hat with the plastic vegetation bobbed and heaved as she made her way to the front of the auditorium. Turning to face the audience, she swept it off her head and offered a deep bow, leaving a partial bouquet on the floor as the hat found a place over her heart. Giggles grew into peals of laughter as Mom began to sing her newest youth camp "special." If you think of the tune to "Battle Hymn of the Republic", you'll get the idea. We all stomped and clapped as she sang. . . .

Mine eyes have seen the horrors of the campers in the dorms
They have shot me with their water guns
They've trampled on my corns
I have my suitcase ready, and I'm waiting for the morn
When I go driving home

Glory, glory, hallelujah, glory, glory, hallelujah
Glory, glory, hallelujah
When I go driving home

I have watched them with their sweethearts
I have seen them smile and wink
I have stuffed their mouths with pillows
I have smelled their socks that stink
My head is getting swimmy
And my heart is on the blink
But I'll soon be driving home

42

"More, more!" cried the stamping, clapping crowd. Chaos reigned in the meeting hall! After several more curtsies and hat sweeps (which left most of the plastic flowers on the floor), Mom launched into yet another crossworded song. This one was crooned to the tune of "The Twelve Days of Christmas". . . .

On the first day of youth camp, my leaders gave to me:
12 sheets of typing
11 said, "No griping"
10 books to keep
9 brooms to sweep
8 rules to teach
7 verses each
6 TY-LEN-OL!
5 broke beds
4 nights to dread
3 eye drops
2 ear stops
And a lumpy bunk on which to sleep!

On the second day of youth camp, the girls gave to me:
12 tons of make-up
11 kids to break up
10 love notes
9 soggy soaps
8 name tags
7 wet rags
6 TY-LEN-OL!
5 split skirts
4 torn shirts

Mom, I'm Telling On You!

3 pairs of dice
2 head lice
And one hour of sleep the whole night through!

On the third day of youth camp, the boys gave to me:
12 pairs of socks
11 hidden rocks
10 water guns
9 knives for fun
8 Cokes stashed
7 bags of trash
6 TY-LEN-OL!
5 radios
4 dirty clothes
3 teddy bears
2 shoes unpaired
And one broken flashlight that was mine!

On the last day of youth camp, misfortune gave to me:
12 kids a-urpin'
11 campers burpin'
10 lost their money
9 lost their honey
8 lost their pens
7 lost their friends
6 TY-LEN-OL!
5 pillow fights
4 busted lights
3 kids a-weepin'
2 kids a-sleepin'
And one lost her mind–and that was me!

Those who weren't holding their sides in laughter were applauding and yelling cheers. The tension was gone. Mom's off key songs were the perfect way to begin a youth camp!

Mom often engaged partners in crime for her nefarious schemes, screams and skits. Among the many chosen (you know who you are) were Sis. Sandra Myer and Sis. Glendale Pate. I'm sure Heaven called for a humor alert every time those three joined forces!

When teaching classes at camp, Mom would often walk the campground looking for "volunteers." If one wanted a permanent spot in the history of youth camps, he simply needed to be a volunteer for one of Mom's capers!

Two particular incidents come to mind, both of which happened at Crusader's Camp, the camp for eight- to eleven-year-old children. The first is the story of Esther and the king who wore tennis shoes, and the second is about a rapture that didn't take place. Enjoy. . . .

The King Who Wore Tennis Shoes

"I will now take for me a new wife," the king roared from his golden throne. Actually the "throne" was a chair covered by Mom's burnt orange bedspread, but the young campers in the audience didn't care. They were captivated. The "throne" sat atop the choir director's raised platform in front of the assembly. Mom had scoured the campgrounds to find a suitable "king" in the form of Jeff Riley, a tall, natural-born comedian. He had "volunteered" for skit duty this day.

Wrapped in yet another bedspread, the king decreed that there would be a beauty contest, and the winner would become his "wife." Campers shouted their approval as the line of available beauties began marching before the king.

"Too short," he said about one beauty, and "I like blondes" culled a few others. The king continued with his wisecracks, eliciting snickers from kids and adults alike. The kids were paying close attention (a feat seldom achieved in a youth camp class), and everyone enjoyed the skit. Even the king was having so much fun that he forgot about his precarious perch on the elevated "box."

"I'll take her," the king shouted, standing to point at "Esther", another volunteer. He stamped his feet for emphasis. But having repeatedly adjusted the golden bedspread before seating himself, he had scooted the throne backward. The throne moved a little *too* far back, with predictable results. The hierarchy toppled backward into the lap of a very surprised lady as both my dad and Esther sought to save him. In the process, his robe flew up to reveal a pair of white tennis shoes kicking and dangling at the end of his long, blue jean clad legs!

Jeff, having been cohort to other Martin antics, lumbered to his feet amid gales of laughter and blurted, "It's a plot; it's a plot! They're trying to kill the king!" The king's court was in total disorder with mirth.

It took a while to settle the setting. After the skit, a tiny girl approached me and said, "That was funny. I liked the part where the king fell down." She paused thoughtfully and continued, "I didn't know that kings wore tennis shoes."

"Neither did I," I replied with a knowing grin.

The Rapture That Didn't Happen

"Today, campers, we are going to talk about something very serious." My dad could look extremely solemn when necessary. It was the last day of camp, and we always tried to have a thought-provoking skit for the kids to remember as they traveled to their homes.

Today was rapture day. The skit would portray a rapture with everyone ascending but one person, who would then give an altar call to end the class. Little did we know that God had ideas of His own that day.

Dad had engineered a system of pulleys and ropes, together with buckets, balloons and white sheets, to represent the saints departing for Heaven. The ceiling of the auditorium where we held class was at least twenty-five feet high with pillars and catwalks for support and maintenance. Dad and a couple of other guilty parties had climbed the poles and rigged a pulley system from the catwalks along the ceiling. Everything tested fine. This one was a sure production.

The lights dimmed, and Dad spoke about the rapture. Then the skit began. The cue for the "rapture" was the loud sound of a trumpet. It blasted exactly on time. Helpers grabbed the ropes and pulled, the spotlight illuminated the correct area, and the children held their breath, expecting the rapture. Nothing happened.

The trumpet sounded anew. Helpers pulled and yanked. Still no rapture. The ropes had caught on something. White, sheet clad figures floated a few feet above ground. Nothing else moved. Silence. Then a little boy spoke.

"Oh, no," he cried. *"They didn't go!"*

The unexpected message swept the crowd, and suddenly God was in control of the service. Dad, feeling a new anointing, told the children that a rapture was surely coming, and if they wanted to go, they must give their hearts to Jesus. Otherwise, they would stay here like those "saints" (floating buckets) in the spotlight. The entire group left their seats and ran to the altar.

After the class was over and the children were dismissed, Dad tested the ropes and found that they worked with no problem.

The Rapture That Didn't Take Place was one of the best skits we were ever a part of, and it taught me the lesson that the only one better at skits than Mom is God!

Tattletales

We might be deprived of paper towels, Kleenex or perfume, but paper plates (of the cheapest variety) squeezed into the budget. We would, in fact, get two of them stuck together for each meal. On the top plate, we ate our main course; then we would pull out the soggy, bottom one for our dessert. This plan works great if you like chocolate cake squatting in grease.

Mom said she always worried, though, about those paper plates. She was afraid we would be eating dinner at a saint's house and would exclaim, "Look, Mom! Their plates don't <u>bend</u> like ours!"

There wasn't a fancy bone in Mama's six-foot frame. Ask anybody who ever came to our house. She would make them comfortable by sitting the pot roast on the table in the big, black skillet. "So it will stay warm," she'd say, but she wasn't fooling us kids. We knew she didn't want to wash extra dishes. She would rather spend that time visiting or writing or playing Boggle . . . or in this case cooking up another bizarre intrigue for the Martin house.

This chapter presents yet another side of Mom: the budding pioneer.

Chapter Six

My Mom, The Pioneer

When we (Dad and I) built our house in Temple, Texas, it sat on the very end of Sumac Street. It was a secluded neighborhood. This meant the Board of Health couldn't find it, and that was a bit of a blessing, too.

In the good old days, we Martin kids had quite a few karate meals. Mom would take everything she could find, chop it up, and throw it on a paper plate for us to wrestle with. Mom could make a meal out of practically anything, and usually she did. Prayers would last awhile at our table because we were serious about them. When we would ask, "What's for supper?" and Mom would say, "Just eat your food and be glad you have it," we all prayed extra.

Most of Mom's meals were delicious (even if we didn't know what they contained). But there were times when Mom felt impressed to save money by making ingredients at home "just like the old pioneers did." Those were her words. I contended that pioneers would have never survived if they had done it Mom's way.

I often rode my bicycle to school. Bonham Junior High was located one mile and two hills from our house. I clearly remember the first signs of the "Pioneer Spirit" as I now call it.

(Back then we called it plenty of other names.) I had just cycled home from school and, like any growing boy, was ravenously hungry, ready to raid the "fridge." I opened the refrigerator door to see three quart jars filled with milk. I loved milk. A lady who attended our church had a Jersey cow, and she sent us raw milk from time to time. Thinking that this was what the jars held, I poured a glass full and took a big gulp.

My yell for help, along with the retching sounds coming from the kitchen, brought Mom running. "What's the matter?" she asked.

"The milk's bad. Real bad," I wheezed, gasping for breath.

"Ha!" Mom laughed. She thought the episode funny. I didn't.

"Whasso funny?" I gargled lemonade, trying to erase the dreadful taste from my mouth.

Mom laughed the harder.

"What is that stuff?" I finally caught my breath.

"It's going to be butter." Mom placed the jar into my hands again. "Here. Shake this while I clean up the sink." I shook as she explained.

"I've found a way to save money," she informed me. "I'm going to start making things at home, like butter and bread and jelly and cottage cheese."

Great, just great, I thought disgustedly. *We'll probably spend all our "savings" on doctor bills.*

Mom launched into a tirade about high prices and bills and pioneers and the fact that years ago they didn't have ready-made things. "We're going back to the good old days."

I shook the jar absently as she delivered her sermonette. Yessirree! We were going back to the old-fashioned, pioneer

52

way of living. Why, she would make all our clothes; we men could cut our own hair. She fairly glowed as she described the marvelous advantages of pioneering. I looked at Dad. He had that "I'm not involved" expression on his face. I knew we were in for trouble.

"We're going to live differently from now on," Mom finished her talk and took the jar from me, popping open the lid. "Butter," she announced. "See?"

"Yuck," I rejoined.

"Get used to it, young man," Mom spoke in her no nonsence voice. "Yep. Things are going to be different around here from now on." Brother, was she ever right!

I wore shirts made of three kinds of polyester. My handmade pants had elastic waists because Mom didn't know how to put in zippers. My sisters had it worse than I, though. Mom could finish a "trailblazer" dress in about an hour and a half. She sewed the girls an entire wardrobe from four different colored pieces of material. They looked like homemade quilts three days a week!

Mom made jelly which wouldn't jell, butter that wouldn't un-jell, homemade bread–and, last but not least, homemade cottage cheese. Do you know what it takes to make cottage cheese? First, she set out milk to spoil (and I mean really spoil) until lumps of stiff milk congregated just underneath the jar lid. Then she removed the lid and poured the whole curdled mess into a diaper. Okay, so it was called cheesecloth; it still looked like a diaper. At this point, she hung the concoction outside so it could drip dry. This part took two or three days.

Imagine the smell of eight pounds of clabbered milk on the front porch, swaying in the evening breeze. Our neighbors scheduled their outdoor activities around Mom's cheese making sessions. The smell was awful and kicked off many discussions between Mom and Dad. My parents had a rule that they would never go to bed while mad at each other, and to my amazement they kept the rule during the cottage cheese days. I think, however, once they had to stay awake for four days and nights to keep that rule.

Not all of Mom's pioneering went awry. We still enjoy the best homemade yeast rolls and "monkey bread" this side of Glory. We didn't have to suffer through *all* of Mom's pioneering; only a portion of the ventures were painful.

After a few months, we returned to "normal" living, and the neighbors resumed their backyard barbecues. However, Mom's pioneer spirit never completely faded. She still pioneered a host of projects. When there was a church fund raiser needing a lady's hand, she was first in line. She started many prayer meetings, and countless new spiritual territories were claimed for Christ by the dedicated trailblazer that is my Mom.

I can see her at the marriage supper of the Lamb, pulling the chief cook to one side and saying, "Listen, I know a way to make some good homemade cottage cheese. Do you want the recipe?" Lord willing, I will be there to give that unfortunate, innocent angel a warning.

Tattletales

Mom's mental gears were different from others'. Her impulses were sometimes flagrant violations of what I considered common sense. At times, I felt that her whims were simply short vacations from sanity when, in fact, they were flashes of sheer brilliance. Most of the time I did not realize this until after the fact . . . or the act.

She used object lessons as teaching tools. Sometimes I knew that I was in the midst of one of those lessons, but often I didn't. Eventually, I got the message. When I had questions, Mom would set me down and tell me a story, using household objects to illustrate her lecture. She made her parables interesting. At times, events transpired during her object lessons that she hadn't planned for.

The story you are about to read is one of those object lessons that got out of hand . . . and almost cost her a toe! It also shows a mother's heart at work. . . .

Chapter Seven

"Toe - Toe - Toenado"

Whoever said, "You can't fool all of the people all of the time" obviously never had to predict Texas weather. I have seen it so hot we kids would have been glad to bob for water instead of apples! Summers are usually dry, but we did have a flood once when Mama tried to fix the kitchen sink.

When there is a storm in Texas, it's usually a bad one. I recall one such storm in Temple after a service in which Dad, the pastor, had called for a rededication of all present. I had not responded, thinking that I might want to try my wings soon. That night lightning struck the house, the wind howled and I promptly reenlisted in God's Army for life!

I have always been more afraid of staying inside than out during a tornado. I figure that if I can see the thing, I at least have a fighting chance of getting away from it. Mama didn't like storms either, so when Dad called from the church one Sunday evening to tell her that a tornado was headed directly for us, she wasted no time getting us into the car.

I need to tell you about this particular car. My father, an excellent mechanic, often purchased different cars at good prices. This car was definitely different! It was a Corvair, which means it fell somewhere between a washing machine and a roller coaster. That is to say, the engine acted like the agitator in Mom's Kenmore top-loader. The little car leaned so far into the corners that one-way signs pointed straight up. Wound up tightly, the tiny jalopy would only travel fifty-five miles per hour. In short, it was not the choice vehicle for running from tornadoes.

"Hurry!" Mom yelled from the front door of the house. The wind was whipping, and thunder rumbled in the distance. I grabbed my jacket–it was almost church time–and ran to the Corvair. Mammoth raindrops began pounding the pavement, and the sky darkened menacingly as Mom opened the door to jump in, forgetting that the opening was somewhat smaller than in most autos.

She slid into the driver's seat shrieking, "Which way is it going?"

"It's coming right for us!" I pointed, terrified.

"Well, let's pray," Mom replied, hurrying to slam the pint-sized door on the old clunker. The door rebounded without closing, allowing the rain to douse her hair as she bent over the steering wheel. "Ouch!" She had caught her foot in the door.

"Oh, God!" She sounded very serious, and for just a moment there was a look of absolute travail on her face. "Oh, God," she repeated for emphasis, "help me. I broke my toe running from this toe-toe-toenado!"

I looked at her again. Her face had changed. She was gasping for breath and . . . *laughing!* Even as she started that washing machine engine and put the roller coaster in gear, she was laughing. We clattered down the road at full throttle as Mama prayed alternately for her broken toe and the toe-toe-toenado and laughed at herself in the meantime!

58

Our prayers were answered that night, for the terrible twister turned another direction, leaving both the house and the church unscathed. We went on to church and had an awesome service. I went on with my life, but it was years before I saw the lesson in the tornado experience. It is this:

If you can laugh at yourself during the storm,
you will never become its victim.

Thanks, Mom, for another marvelous object lesson from the heart–and the toe!

Tattletales

When I was about ten years old, Mom became a secret agent of a unique sort, an agent of love who helped each of us kids to feel that he or she was her favorite child. The great secret of Mom's "special" love was kept for years. In fact, I didn't unravel the mystery until just before writing this book. Can you keep a secret? Okay, I'll tell you about it. . . .

Chapter Eight

Mom Was a Secret Agent

Mom would have made a good CIA agent. The Lord knows she was an excellent spy. How she found out about our shenanigans still amazes me, as well as some others who thought they had outsmarted her. She was a great detective and an even better "undercover operative." She accomplished many a grand scheme under the cover of that mischievous grin she sported. And she had her own secret codes, too. She called them words.

Mom loved words. The bigger they were–and the more weird sounding–the better she liked them. If she didn't have one, she'd simply invent one. These were her own code words, some of which we never deciphered!

During the Christmas season one year, she was determined to surprise each of us kids with his or her gift, so she communicated with Dad in "Spanish." We were determined to break her secret code in order to learn what we were getting. Whatever this object was, she called it a "frijole bagita." How it was spelled, we hadn't a clue.

We took the secret message to school and presented it to the Spanish teacher. What, for crying out loud, was a frijole bagita? The teacher looked puzzled. She frowned in deep thought and said she had *never* heard of a frijole bagita. Was it perhaps a dialect she didn't know? she wondered. Indeed it was. It was Mama's secret code.

Mom won. It wasn't until Christmas that we learned. Frijole bagita was her "Spanish" for "bean bag"!

Mom also carried out secret assignments. We kids didn't know about them for a long time; in fact, she was never caught on any of her covert missions, proving that she was indeed a superior secret agent. The story that follows is true and complete to the best of my knowledge:

On grocery shopping day, I–the firstborn– knew I was Mom's favorite child. It was an indisputable fact.

On grocery shopping day, Angella–the middle child–knew she was Mom's favorite child. It was an indisputable fact.

On grocery shopping day, Bethany–the youngest child–knew she was Mom's favorite child. It was an indisputable fact.

Recently, I uncovered Mom's strategy for making each of us feel like king of the mountain. She confessed.

"Psst! C'mere!" Mom's urgent whisper called me to my bedroom door. I opened it, and her hand shot toward me, a mysterious parcel in its grip.

"Hurry, take it." I took the small, green package and looked at it.

"It's for you. Just for you. Hide 'em, and don't tell anybody. I got 'em special just for you!" The green candy wrapper from the grocery store proclaimed that "Andes Mints" were the best anywhere. I knew that. They were my favorite candy. I loved them but seldom got them.

Dad was pastor of a very small but wonderful church flock, most of which worked hard for a living. With no millionaires in our church (at least, we didn't know about it if there were), the tithes which were supposed to support our family and pay our bills didn't. Therefore, Dad worked two and sometimes three extra jobs to make ends meet. We never had extra money, and when we did, it always seemed to be spent on parts for one of the three or four odd–and I do mean odd–cars or trucks Dad tried to keep on the road. Between the vehicles and the electric bill, there were very few fringe benefits.

Grocery shopping day was the only exception to the poverty rule, at least for me. Around the first of every month, Mom went grocery shopping. If you think you know all about grocery shopping, you have never gone to the store with LaJoyce Martin. If Mom asks you to go to the food store with her, you need to plan for an expedition. The trek requires two different colored pencils, some scrap paper, a calculator with spare batteries, food (unless Mom's cohort wants to fast all day), an extra purse or paper sack and a box of Kleenex. These items are essential to a person's well-bring while shopping with Mother.

I always found a vital task to do around the house on food day. I was not conditioned for eight hours of checking nutrition labels, restacking items in shopping carts and staring at Kroger's Pro hamburger meat, which was mostly soybean with a few ounces of beef thrown in.

Mom often went alone on these sojourns while the rest of us sat at home and tried to guess what she would bring to our kitchen. She was and still is the only woman on earth who can turn twenty-five dollars into an entire cart full of edibles.

We were midway through Dad's fifth year as pastor of

Mom, I'm Telling On You!

Midway United Pentecostal Church in Temple, Texas, when I suddenly discovered that I was Mom's beloved descendant. I knew this because I received the secret gifts of candy once a month without fail. Every time Mom snuck into my room, I felt more special and more loved than anyone else.

I suppose I will never realize the sacrifices that were made for those small, foil wrapped packages. Mom was adept at hiding the hard times from us kids. I remember instances when Dad would confront Mom about money spent.

"I thought you were going to buy some new hairpins this time," he would remark.

"Umm," Mom would glance at me or one of my sisters. "I had something else I needed to get." Those glances told Dad where the extra money had gone.

"But, honey," he would protest, "you need those hairpins."

Mom would set her mouth firmly and reply, "Not as much as I needed that other thing."

I remember goodies appearing in my room almost by magic: little trinkets that I wanted desperately but knew we couldn't afford. Mom never seemed to need new clothes or shoes like other women, but we kids constantly found the perfect gift sitting on our beds just when we needed it most.

Above everyone else in our halfway house, I knew I was loved by Mom and Dad. Through the chills and thrills of childhood and into my terrible teens, those little, green packages were evidences of Mom's love. Even after I left home and went to Bible school, the small gifts continued. I finally found the woman of my dreams and married; together we have lived an active and fulfilled life. Recently I opened my mailbox to find yet another gift from my mom.

Through the years I began to understand a child's need to feel valuable and to share a secret bond with his parents. This attachment is the cement that connects families in the most stressful of times, and Mom was a professional at keeping her brood glued together.

As I talked with her in preparation for writing this book, the subject of Mom's secret gifts surfaced again. I laughed as I told her how important I felt because she was buying them solely for me.

"Oh, but you weren't the only one getting special gifts." Mom smiled as she revealed her latest secret. "You see, I was getting each of my children one special gift every month. I told all three of you not to tell anyone else. That way you would feel special. Each person's gift was different from the others'."

No, they weren't, I thought as I sat remembering them one by one. *They were all the same.* I had just discovered that a mother's love, although wrapped in diverse bundles, remains unchanging. *Love* was the gift my parents gave exclusively to each of us children, and Mom was the secret agent who delivered it.

Tattletales

Mom communicated with us children in a language we could understand. She was lively and colorful when making a point. Often she called on Heavenly help when delivering her sermonettes. One particular occasion called for a host of angry angels as cast for Mom's dramatic oration. . . .

Chapter Nine

The Rock Concert

My sisters were too young to remember much about the traveling days, but I was nine years old when we settled down. I have acute memory (and some that isn't so cute) of those evangelistic years. Mom calls them priceless because, she jokes, we didn't get paid. Our most prosperous year netted $2000 after paying for gasoline.

Mom made the most of the least and the best of the worst, and I was too young and happy to know the difference. Take, for instance, the truly fun place we stayed during a revival in Texas. Never mind trying to figure out where it was; the church is no longer in existence.

The congregation consisted of the preacher's family and one elderly lady who tugged on Mom's skirt one night and croaked, "It's a bit short, don't you think?" The skirt was amply long.

The lodging provided for us was an unfinished hull miles into the "boonies," complete with grass burs, dirt roads and barbed wire. The place was so primitive that I was amazed the one naked light bulb hanging from the ceiling wasn't a wind-up model! We thanked God it was summer when we took our baths in the back yard under the water faucet. On second thought, we didn't thank God too loudly for summer, for we had no air conditioning and no screens on the windows to deter the bugs. Dad shot some edible birds, and we roasted them over an open fire outside. (I am not exaggerating!)

But now for the fun part. Someone had built a totally awesome trolley with a cable and a pipe. It ran from a tall tree to the ground. To ride, all one had to do was climb to the very top of the barn, get a handgrip on the pipe and slide all the way to the earth beneath. It was wonderful!

Mom was terrified, but what a sport she was! She didn't show a moment's fear as she climbed the ladder to the top of the barn and wrapped her hands around the piece of pipe. Dad and I were standing at the bottom to cheer her on.

Here she came, skirts flying . . . but lo, her generous weight made the cable sag. The pipe crawled to a stop, leaving her dangling.

"Help me! Honey, help me!" she yelped at my dad.

"Just let go, LaJoyce!" he bellowed back.

"I can't; I'll fall!" Mom wailed.

We–Dad and I–held our sides, laughing. Mom's feet were almost touching the ground, but she didn't know it. Her eyes were shut as tightly as a clam. She had been too scared to ride down with them open.

I think there were many times when Mom shut her eyes, especially to the faults of others. One of those times was the rock concert, a story about a stubborn, young boy and a mom who could see no evil. . . .

"Mom!" I shouted at the top of my lungs, bursting into the kitchen where my mother was busy cooking supper for a family of five.

"Mom, guess what? My band teacher just asked me to play for the Polyfonics. They make records and everything! They're awesome. He wants me to play the bass guitar for them." The excited words tumbled over themselves as I spilled the good news.

"Who," my mom wanted to know, "are the Polyfonics?"

The Polyfonics were major league, cool stuff for a fifteen-year-old. They traveled and played in large auditoriums, and they produced records. They were popular; everyone at school thought the Polyfonics were supercalifragilisticexpiali-docious.

I tried to explain all this to Mom. They played at all of the school's major functions, took part in the most fun activities and were scheduled to cut another record soon.

"We'll think about it, son," she promised me.

All right, I thought, *she didn't say no!* Mom and Dad were great parents, but sometimes grown-ups can dampen good times, at least from a kid's point of view. I just *had* to play for the Polyfonics. It would be a dream come true!

"We'll talk about it in the morning," Mom promised after I had pestered her all through supper.

Mom always set the alarm clock by her bed. She said it gave her something to ignore. I trust you are getting the picture that Mom wasn't a morning person. Thus it was almost noon when Mom made her appearance in the living room where I sat anxiously waiting.

"All right. Let's talk." Mom sat on one end of the couch, and I on the other. I started to speak, but she raised her hand for silence.

"First, let's pray," she said. That had been bothering me all morning. Mom always prayed when she made a decision about one of us kids. Most of the time that was good, but on this occasion I wasn't sure. Mom didn't know all about the Polyfonics yet, but I did. I had made it a point to gather all the information I could, and there were several details about the group that I knew would not meet with Mom's approval. I had hoped to wiggle around the sensitive points and give her enough "good stuff" to get her blessing.

"Kneel," she commanded. I knelt. While Mom launched into a first-class, "help me do the right thing" prayer, I did a little lobbying of my own. *God,* I pled, *I enjoy the simple pleasures of life, but every once in a while I enjoy a biggie thrown in there, too. This means everything to me. Please, let her say yes!* My prayer continued along those lines for five minutes until Mama ran out of steam and sat up.

"Now," she said, "tell me about these Polyfonics. What type of music do they play?" That was one of the subjects I'd hoped to avoid. Mom insisted on music that was completely wholesome and not connected in any way with rock music or her version of it. The problem was, her version of rock music was anything with a) loud drums, b) a lead guitar louder than the vocals, c) lyrics that weren't traditional or gospel and d) anything we wouldn't listen to if Jesus Christ was standing beside us. That really narrowed the field and positively took the "Poly" and most of the "fonics" out of the school band in question.

"Well, they're really cool, Mom. They play all sorts of easy listening music." By easy listening I meant it was easy for teenagers to listen to. It seemed that my definition of rock music and Mom's differed substantially. However, being aware that I might face this question, I had prepared.

"Mom, I have their latest record. Why don't you come

into my room and hear it?" Mom said she would be there in a minute. I bounded to my room to find the slowest, softest song on the record. Punching the power button on my hundred and fifty watt J.C. Penney stereo, I carefully placed the record onto the turntable and set the needle on its edge.

I was across the room and reaching for my bass guitar to play along when I remembered the volume knob. Normally, I liked my music loud. This time was an exception. I dove for the stereo, but it was too late. A strong bass rhythm filled the room, and a screaming lead guitar wound into a contemporary music introduction. I reached the volume control and desperately turned it counterclockwise but not in time. Footsteps resounded in the hall, and Mom burst into my room.

"Turn that off right now!" Mom demanded.

"But, Mom," I yelled, "I haven't even found the song I want you to hear!"

"I've heard enough," she declared, dragging me to my bedroom window.

"Look," she ordered. I looked out at the windblown trees that dotted our lawn.

"What?" I retorted belligerently.

"See those angels out there?" I didn't, but it mattered not a whit to her. She was on a roll and would not be stopped.

"Those are our guardian angels, Kevin, and when you started playing that awful music, I saw them packing to leave. They're leaving, Kevin, because of that horrid music!" I didn't believe her. Suddenly I was mad. Madder than I had been in many months.

"This is the thing I've worked for and wanted all my life!" I shouted. "I've practiced and studied and learned, and now that I have my chance, you tell me I can't do it. What kind of parent is that, huh? Tell me!" The ranting lasted for some time as Mom grew quieter and quieter. Finally, she walked out and left me with my self pity turning to shame. Mom really did care for me, I knew, and I'd just said some hateful things to her.

As I stared out the window, looking for angels with suitcases in hand, it became clear to me. The real guardian angel was the one I'd sent packing with my angry words. I began that day to appreciate Mom's dedication to us kids. She discovered the good and turned the other cheek–and a blind eye–to the rest.

A few hours later after apologizing and being forgiven, I asked my mom if she had truly seen angels.

"Well, maybe not," she smiled down at me, "but I'm looking at one now." Boy, talk about seeing no evil!

Tattletales

Mom frequently quoted the scripture that says faith without works is dead. "Put some legs on them prayers!" she'd admonish. She practiced what she preached, too, especially where money was concerned. She aided God by saving every penny she could.

This story is about Mom's famous "Super Saver" days and about coupons and the many blessings (and "blastings") that accompanied them. . . .

Chapter Ten

Been There, Done That, Got The T-Shirt (All at Half the Price!)

In every aspect of life, Mom's gender showed. She knew absolutely nothing about cars, lawn mowers or boys' toys. For the girls, she could create an amazing doll–complete with arms, legs, head and body–from a handkerchief. But when it came to making a kite, well, . . . let's just say she never made one that would fly. Perhaps the big knots in the rag tail were too heavy. Or maybe the flour and water paste wouldn't hold the paper to the frame. Or it could have been that the whole thing was woefully out of proportion.

Run against the wind as I might, holding the string, the pitiful contraption would make a few, crazy loops and nosedive straight into the ground. It isn't a wonder that she turned the kite business to Dad.

Nor could she master the game of chess. She would try to play for hours, becoming more and more frustrated when her opponents gobbled her men. Finally, she realized the game wasn't for her when she knelt to pray, closed her eyes and began moving rooks and knights and bishops in her mind. That's when she gave it up forever and went back to playing jacks with the girls.

But she was a dead shot with a gun. Dad claimed she could pick a rabbit out of a field with one bullet. He said it was because she didn't flinch no matter how hard the gun kicked. However, hunting wasn't her cup of tea, so she surrendered the gun to Dad once and for all.

She preferred her pencil and paper, her crochet needle, her recipe for apple dumplings or her coupons. Someone (I have forgotten just who) introduced Mom to coupons in the late seventies, and the world changed again for us Martins.

When it came to shopping, Mom was at least fifty percent off. What I mean to say is that she didn't buy unless she could save money on her purchases. Mom was frugal, to say the least. She learned that unpopular cuts of meat cost less, so she dug to the bottom of the stack and pulled them out. Have you ever eaten ankle of pork before? That was living "high on the hog" for us! Most kids hunted Easter eggs to get a prize. We Martin kids hunted Easter eggs to get the eggs, or so it seemed to me!

Mom learned to shop the thrift stores, garbage sales (this is not a misprint), flea markets and any other place that slashed prices, gleaning those few precious items her family could use. Five dollars could buy us a wholly or partially new wardrobe. When we went on vacation, Mom would produce "new" T-shirts for everyone. Instead of "Disney World" or "Six Flags", ours might proclaim "St. Luke's Marathon for Charity" or some other such nonsense, but we kids couldn't have cared less. We were happy to have them.

Mom's coupons gained us motel rooms with five dollars off a night, discount tickets to the petting zoo and free french fries at McDonalds. The Martin clan could truly say, "We have been there, done that and got the T-shirt," all for at least half the price.

She saved money at every opportunity, but she saved the most in people's garages and at the food stores. Years ago in Temple, grocery stores would periodically advertise "Double Coupon" discounts. For example, the store would double a customer's twenty-five cent coupon, and the shopper would save fifty cents. That was before Mom arrived. At one of those stores, she spent thirty-five dollars and saved seventy-four; many products she obtained completely free. Needless to say, that store went out of business after a while (we still think Mom contributed to its demise).

She clipped coupons from every newspaper, magazine and tabloid available. There were coupons on the kitchen table, in plastic sandwich bags over the stove and almost everywhere else you can imagine.

As her addiction grew, it became hard to decipher which coupon was to be used for each article, so Dad bought her an expandable coupon file with tabs from A to Z. That way the coupons could be lost in alphabetical order.

The coupon craze caught hold, and Mom began saving even more money. We took half-priced vacations on the funds Mom salvaged with those coupons!

The extra wealth and savings were great. In fact, there was only one problem with Mama's coupon compulsion. We didn't always like the product touted by the newest savings stub. Some items were simply too gross to eat.

Mom, I'm Telling On You!

We dropped delicate hints to Mom, trying not to hurt her feelings, but she never seemed to understand our implications. She'd grab the overstuffed suitcase she called a purse, tie on her favorite shopping scarf and march to our old Pontiac, ready to ambush yet another unsuspecting store.

I need to clear up any confusion. Mom did have a method to her madness. She would wait until things were on a clearance sale, and then she'd barge in and demand her double coupon discount. It's a wonder the store didn't pay her after her groceries were checked!

After spending three or four hours gathering her half-priced or less treasures, she'd parade up to the checkout stand. Woe is the poor, unwitting checker who looked up to see Mom standing in line! I always joked that Mom had a favorite checker at Safeway, one of the local supermarkets. I knew which one she was by looking at her fingertips. They had callouses on them from ringing up Mom's coupons.

After the store had been duly raided and plundered and the shelves left in shock from the aftermath of Mom's ambuscade, we became the next victims. Mom would pull to the curb in front of our house and honk the horn, which meant, "Everybody come out and help unload the loot." We would all troop out and drag in a carload of sacks and boxes. Then came the fun part.

Mom would begin taking out the items and showing them around like trophies. "I got this box of oatmeal for eight cents!" she would crow, beaming at us.

"Oh, and this," she indicated an outdated pie crust, "was only a nickel. And here are some generic green beans I got free, and this string was three cents."

Mom's zeal often ran ahead of her good sense where

coupons were concerned, so our post-shopping household conversations went something like this. . . .

"And these," Mom would gush, "are falafels. I got six boxes!"

"Mom?"

"Huh?"

"What are falafels?"

"Well, you know, something to eat . . ."

"What do they taste like?"

"Well, I don't know. I got 'em free. You don't have to eat 'em; Daddy and I will eat 'em." My dad is still alive; however, he seemed to age rather quickly during those years. Coupons were a great part of our family entertainment then, and to this day my mother remains a coupon junkie.

Another bargain Mom was "into" was generic items. Those cans all look alike and have yellow paper labels. Here is a tip from someone who has been there: Be sure to read each generic label carefully before you taste the contents. Cat food and refried beans look quite similar.

Then stores began selling bent cans. You could get a bent container of something for a nickel or a dime. Often nothing was wrong with the contents other than their being under a little extra pressure. You can imagine the excitement that sometimes caused!

Some of the bent cans had no labels, so Mom learned the codes stamped into the bottoms. She could tell the contents of almost any can by deciphering the "can code." A few codes, though, proved to be deceptive. One such can had "PM" stamped on the bottom. Dad and I ate two sandwiches made from its contents, which we took to be potted meat, before Mom figured out we were eating Puppy-Mix.

Mom, I'm Telling On You!

As time went on, Mom expanded her shopping escapades to include garage sales. They also remain another of Mom's addictions. I firmly believe that she will "shop till she drops," looking for just one more steal of a deal. Mom is such a bargain hunter that I often wonder what she'll do in Heaven. If there are garage sales, I imagine the scene will look something like this:

"Pardon me, sir, but could you give me directions to the Disciples' Square?" LaJoyce Martin parks her chariot in the middle of Glory Avenue, oblivious to the traffic jam she is precipitating on the golden streets of Heaven.

"You see, I saw this garage sale advertised in the *New Jerusalem Times*, and I'm most eager to arrive early to look over the items listed."

"Follow me." The archangel thrusts his chariot into first gear and roars off in a cloud of exhilarating exhaust that smells even better than an Avon bottle collection on earth.

At Disciples' Square, he points directly to the garage of Matthew, the once earthly tax collector. Obviously, he is still collecting in Heaven though not in taxes.

Ah! This is Heaven all right. Heaven just wouldn't be complete without garage sales! And such an array!

A stack of used halos occupies the first table.

"Let's see, now," the Mrs. Martin murmurs, calculating quickly. "If I can buy a few of those used halos at a reduced price and sell them for a higher price, I can take that cruise down the River of Life with the Prophets to attend the National Convention come September. . . ."

She fingers the used halos, a faraway, rapturous gleam in her eyes. They are all sizes and in all stages of deterioration.

A little spray paint, some glue, a bit of straightening here and there . . . But to whom could she sell used halos?

Ah, yes! Those earthly saints would give her a good price for one just in case they had not been able to pay for a new one on their own merits. She'd set up a booth or, at least, hang a sign at Heaven's gate and catch them just as they came in.

Three used halos are carefully laid to one side as the thrilling browsing continues. Golden slippers! Size 4½. Pretty small, but surely they'll fit somebody. Maybe one of the grandkids could wear them. Too good a buy to pass up. It isn't every day one finds golden slippers, nearly new, at a garage sale and at such a reasonable price!

A whole rack of robes–all sizes and shapes! One big enough to fit Elroy. It's a bit frayed at the border, but a little turning of the hem will fix that. Let's see. . . . Who else needs a robe? A little bleach . . .

The truth is dawning upon Matthew; he has a brilliant idea.

"Lady, I'll sell you the whole kit and caboodle at a real bargain, and you can have your own garage sale."

"Sold!" exclaims Mrs. Martin, breathlessly excited. And boxes and boxes and hours and hours later, her chariot is full to the brim with goodies, and she departs for her own fair mansion with soaring spirits to get her sale underway.

Some days later, a newcomer to Heaven stops the same archangel mid-street and asks, "Pardon me, sir, but could you direct me to the mansion of one Fern LaJoyce Berry Martin? According to the *New Jerusalem Times*, she is throwing a gigantic garage sale."

"Follow me." The angel shoves his chariot into high

gear and streaks away. At the Martin Mansion, he pauses and points before returning to his heavenly business.

The newcomer alights, ascends the celestial steps to the mansion and notices a small note pinned to the front door's screen with a golden bobby pin:

GONE TO NATIONAL CONVENTION
WITH THE PROPHETS.

GARAGE SALE POSTPONED
UNTIL SPRING.

F. L. B. M.

TATTLETALES

From her early teens, Mom had a special gift of relating to children. As her proficiency increased over the years, church camp organizers began to request her talents for their youth camps and children's activities, and pastors began to ask her to bring her ministries to their congregations for Sunday School promotions, rallies and seminars. Mom tried to reach every boy and girl she met. Several of those youngsters grew to be preachers, evangelists and missionaries.

The fact that she survived the incidents related in this next chapter is living proof that she loved children . . . particularly us crazy Martin kids.

Chapter Eleven

Mud Pickles

Mom was bad about giving away secrets. Especially God's secrets. None of us ever figured out how she knew what was going on in Heaven at any given time, but we knew better than to question her ESP. Here's a sample:

There was a knock on God's office door. A massive angel stood patiently waiting.

"Priority mail," the angel said when God appeared. The Lord didn't bat an eye. He was used to letters and telegrams and faxes and 911 calls.

"From where?"

"Arizona, Texas, Oklahoma, Arkansas, New Mexico, Colorado . . ."

"So many letters?"

"Only one, Sir."

"Now, Happy Halo—"

"The sender seems to be a nomad, Sir."

"Be a little more specific, please. Who sent the message?"

The angel adjusted his bifocals. "Let's see. Elroy and LaJoyce M–a–r— Martin."

"Martin. I know them. They're My children, and they love Me. They do travel a lot, doing My work."

"Shall I open the letter for You, Lord?"

"No, I'll open My own mail."

The angel fluttered from one wing to the other, wanting to be on his way but held by an angel's insatiable curiosity. "Well, what's so important as to warrant priority mail, Lord? It costs extra postage for that, You know."

"Hmmm. This couple has put in a special request. They've been married for nigh to five years, and they want some little Martins in their nest."

"Just a minute, Lord. Isn't that the couple you have scheduled to travel for nine years? Didn't You say—?"

"You're right."

"Of course, You'll have to tell them no."

"Not so fast, Happy Halo. They were brave enough to ask, so their petition shall be granted."

"Just like that?"

"Just like that. Pick out the most precious, little soul you can find and get it ready to ship to earth."

"Do You have a preference, Lord? Boy or girl?"

"Let's make it a boy first, and save two girls for later."

The angel put his wings into overdrive. "This is so exciting, Lord! Can I have a little part in the ceremony when he gets there–like writing a poem or something?"

"No, Happy Halo. It's not that I don't trust your rhymes, but we'll leave that job to his Grandpa Berry. He's been writing poems for years."

Suddenly the angel's smile faded. "God, aren't You taking a terrible risk stuffing another human in that back model, single axle, seventeen foot travel trailer? Why, it's even smaller than seventeen feet inside!"

God looked amused. "Haven't you learned by now, Happy Halo, that with Me there are no risks? Now, get on with your job. I'm sure they'll do their job well. . . ."

Mom added the derby of "mother" to the many other hats she wore with apparent ease. After all, would you talk back to a six-foot-four matriarch? Most times the household was happy and somewhat stress-free. However, there were a few hiccups along the way, most of them provided by yours truly and the two sisters.

One such catastrophe occurred in that little trailer we called the Dumpster. The church we were helping had a generous saint who would bring us groceries in gallon cans. We had gallons of beans, corn, hominy, turnip greens (that can could last forever), and ketchup. Ketchup was my favorite food seasoning. I loved it on just about everything, and for once we had plenty of it.

The wide-mouthed cans were hard to pour from, so Mom got a funnel and transferred the ketchup into milk jugs. Those jugs proved to be perfect one-gallon ketchup bottles–except for one thing. The lids came off too easily. Mom knew that, but I didn't.

Everyone knows that ketchup tastes better when shaken first. Any eight-year-old kid can tell you that. I cannot recollect exactly what it was we were about to eat, but it needed ketchup–shaken up ketchup–on it. Sitting at our boomerang shaped table, full of youthful wisdom and ready to eat, I grabbed the ketchup bottle and prepared to—

"Kevin, don't shake that ketchup." *What?* Didn't Mom know that ketchup must be shaken to be good?

"But, Mom, it has to be shook. It's better that way!" I protested while lifting the jug.

"Kevin Martin, I said, 'Don't shake that ketchup bottle.' Did you hear me?"

"But, Mom!" This was getting serious! What was Mom thinking? I *had* to shake it.

"Victor Kevin Martin, if you shake that ketchup bottle, the lid will come off and ketchup will go everywhere. And if you think I will be happy about that, *you've got another think coming!*"

Mom was always giving me another think coming. But this time she must be wrong. The lid was on, and it wasn't coming off. I would prove it to her.

"Aw, Mom, it won't come off. See, it—" It *did* come off. And, you know what, Mom was right. Ketchup went everywhere on me, on the table, and all over the snowy white curtains that Mom had recently hung. It even got on the ceiling of the Dumpster. There was a beat of breathless silence as Mom stopped and stared. I sat there with her simply looking at me . . . and had my other think coming.

Most kids are good at getting their way. Most kids are experts at playing parents against each other. Most kids can figure a way to get what they want and still have parents. Of course, there's most kids, and then there's my sister, Angella.

Angella is the middle child. She is five and a half years younger than me, and the more I saw of her, the more convinced I became that I was never her age. She could act dreadful and the next minute be as sweet as pie.

Angella enjoyed music. She enjoyed listening to it, clapping, humming and singing, but mostly she enjoyed making music. At the writing of this book, she is an accomplished vocalist with a music degree. At five years old, though, she had not yet attained the art of making her noises joyful.

Someone who liked (or hated) the Martin clan thought that we needed an instrument of fine art in our halfway house and sold Dad a large, upright piano for the playroom. The fifty dollar monstrosity was almost irreparable, but Dad was determined to make it work. After several days of intensive repair on the felts and hammers and hand tuning the old strings, the gargantuan monument to fine arts was available for use. Ready for music it might have been, but no one could have prepared it for Angella.

Remember that I said most kids are good at playing one parent against the other? Angella could give post-graduate lessons in third-party manipulation! She was a genius at using one parent to get to the other. On frequent occasions this talent worked in her favor, but once in a while it backfired as it did on this particular day.

After a few weeks of having kids pound on it, the "new" piano became old to my parents. So they instituted practice times and gave each of us equal opportunity on the instrument. For the most part, this worked beautifully until the day Angella decided she would use a week's worth of practice time all at once.

Angella only knew one song. An enterprising pianist in our church had taught her a tune played only on the black keys entitled "I Dropped My Dolly in the Dirt." This song is excellent for its intended use, which is to familiarize piano students with sharps and flats on the piano keyboard. It was never intended to be the sole tune of a three hour concert.

Mom had become distracted with some important

project of the day, and Dad was busy working on one of our several vehicles that required constant maintenance. The garage where all the mechanic work went on was, incidentally, adjacent to the playroom where the piano sat.

Angella took advantage of the hubbub to stage a concert. The concert began lightly and gathered volume, remaining uninterrupted in full magnitude for quite some time. Finally, the repetitive notes pounded at full volume began to take their toll on Dad.

"Angella," he called from his position under the hood of our car, "that's enough. No more piano for today, okay?" No answer. Silence lasted a few seconds before the same song started up again.

"Angella, did you hear me?" The song continued without pause. Dad extricated himself from his tools and engine parts and marched into the house.

"Angella, did you hear me? I said, 'Stop.'"

"But, Daddy, I'm playing 'I Dropped My Dolly in the Dirt.' I have to play for the concert!"

"Young lady," which is what Dad called my sister when she wasn't being one, "if you play 'I Dropped My Dolly in the Dirt' one more time, you're going to get a spanking. Do you hear me?" As this was said at full volume, there was no doubt that Dad had been heard.

Blessed silence descended on the house for a few, short minutes, but then softly, slowly the plaintive notes began again, "I–dropped–my—" Dad dropped his tools, washed his hands and headed for the playroom and Angella.

"Angella, did I not tell you specifically not to play 'I Dropped My Dolly in the Dirt' again? Did I?" Angella knew she was in serious trouble, so she put on her most innocent, cherubic face and slowly turned toward Dad.

"But, Daddy," she said pitifully, "I wasn't playing 'I Dropped My Dolly in the Dirt.' I was playing 'I Dropped My *Pickle* in the Dirt'!" Dad went to tell Mom about the new song. They had a good laugh in private; then together they went to stop the concert.

Bethany was the youngest. In many households, the youngest gets away with the most mischief, but in Mom's and Dad's house, nobody got away with much. The girls shared a room sporting a walk-in closet with separate doors, a single dresser and a pastry shaped bed that Angella had dreamed up. The bed was sculpted exactly like a wedge of pie, and my sisters were its filling. Mom topped the whole confection with pie-shaped sheets and bedspread.

You would think that girls would spend their time playing with dolls on their cute bed, but we're talking about my sisters and not just any girls. My sisters added a new dimension to doll playing. Most of their talking dolls had been baptized in water so many times that they simply blubbered. These girls liked action! They wanted drama and excitement, and they went to great lengths to find it.

Bethany loved playing in the closet among the clothes, the hangers and the shoes. She would spend hours there, playing house or store or church. But sometimes playing church or house was just too tame. She invented more exciting amusements.

The afternoon was long and begged to be filled with fun, so Bethany (with the help of Angella and a cousin near her age) found a solution. The room was noisy, but as noise was common among us kids, Mom paid it no mind. It wasn't until she went into the room to find something in the girls' closet that she noticed something amiss. Opening the door brought instant silence. Angella and her cousin turned stricken eyes toward Mother, who was rapidly becoming angry.

The closet had been plundered and ravaged until it was hardly recognizable. Not one piece of clothing was left on the hangers; everything had been thrown helter-skelter into the closet floor. As if that was not enough, every wire hanger had been tangled and twisted into an unidentifiable heap. Dolls' heads were removed and arms and legs strewn amid shoes, socks and other debris.

Mom's eyes lifted to the shelf above the clothes rod. Perched high above the rubble was Bethany. Mom, taking it all in, asked one of her favorite "you're really in trouble" questions.

"What on earth do you think you're doing?" There was lightning in her eyes and thunder in her voice. The sisters were frozen as they tried to figure a way out of looming punishment.

Finally Bethany looked down at Mom and said, "We didn't mean to do anything wrong. We were just playing tornado!"

At that moment I'm sure it took all of Mom's love to overcome the urge to adopt us out for a lifetime.

Amidst the many trials of motherhood, Mom proved her love for her children over and again. She finally raised her brood to adulthood, and one by one we left to seek our fortunes. However, her love has continued through each and every moment of our lives.

She was in her fifties before she "grandmothered," and when news of the prospect came, her crochet needles flew into warp speed. Probably no child ever had more crocheted booties in a size pre-zero.

When my wife, Karen, and I produced her first grandchild, she was on hand to see the job well done. Believe me, the doctor knew she was there!

Sometime later, she authored this cute allegory:

In the beginning, God created Cherish Rose Martin. And the babe was without fault or flaw.

And God said, "Let there be delight," and there was delight. And God saw delight, that it was good. And the evening and the morning were the first day.

And God said, "Let there be people in the midst of the hospital room to visit." Some smiled, and some wept for joy. These he called grandparents. And the evening and the morning were the second day.

And God divided the day from the night, but Cherish Rose Martin didn't know it yet. She ruled the night as well as the day. And her father said, "This is not so good; I have to work tomorrow!"

And God blessed them, and her father said, "We'll be grateful and replenish the bank account and have dominion over the diaper bag." And God saw the couple that He had made into a family, and behold, it was very good. And the evening and the morning was Friday, July 20. And God rested, but the parents didn't.

And it came to pass in the process of time that Grandmother LaJoyce Martin had a wonderful thought in the midst of her mind, and this is the conclusion of her whole matter:

Though I had a nice home and new car and had not Cherish Rose Martin, I would be incomplete and feel a great emptiness.

Mom, I'm Telling On You!

Though I had the money for baby gifts to give others and gave booties and blankets and sleeping gowns and had not my own Cherish Rose, I would not be satisfied.

Though I bestowed all sorts of goodies on my nieces and nephews and babysat them often, it profited me nothing in comparison with my own Cherish Rose.

Other babies may be sweet; other babies may be pretty. But my grandbaby is special to me.

Mine is never too much trouble, will never be too big or too little to fit inside my heart. She will never be too young or too old to draw from my store of love.

For her we are willing to bear all things, spend all things, do all things, believe all things, hope all things and endure all things because love for one's grandchild never faileth. Whether there be affection from classmates, it shall fail. Whether there be love from friends, it might cease. Whether there be friendly neighbors, they shall vanish away.

For they are not a part of us like Cherish Rose. But now we have that missing part, and we love that part. The essence of perfect love has come into our hearts.

When my son and daughter-in-law were a couple, they spoke as a couple, they understood as a couple, they thought as a couple. But when they became parents, they put away their status as a couple and became a family.

Now abideth these three generations, but we know the greatest of all is our God who gave us this blessing.

—The Gospel Acording to LaJoyce Martin
Chapter One

Tattletales

In the philosophy of life, LaJoyce Martin believed that destiny shapes our end–and calories end our shapes. Mom was "into" dieting. And whatever she got into, the whole family got into. This was her idea of support for her diets. There were some healthy side effects to her weight watching obsessions. It is difficult to get heartburn while eating cold cuts three meals a day!

Mom gave dieting her best and our best, too! This book wouldn't be complete without a few examples of her ignoble slim down programs.

Chapter Twelve

Weighed . . .
and Found Wanting

Bathroom scales and Mom didn't get along. She hated them and would have had them banned from Wal-Mart if she'd had the executive power.

One session with the scales in the morning and her nerves were wrecked. She was depressed for the remaining 23 hours and 59 minutes of the day.

She didn't have a digital scale; she had the old-fashioned kind that was adjustable. All we kids would have had to do was sneak in her bathroom and run the dial in reverse past zero about ten notches. We could have had a perfect day complete with cake and ice cream to celebrate her weight "loss." It's a pity we didn't learn that bit of diplomacy in infancy.

Was there ever a diet that Mom didn't try? There was the garlic toast and avocado diet. It was so effective that Mom breathed out her garlic like Saul of Tarsus breathed out his threatenings. We couldn't stand her, and she couldn't stand herself. (She was losing friends instead of pounds.)

Then there was the white tuna and Gouda cheese diet.

Mom, I'm Telling On You!

She lost forty pounds that year–and gained fifty the next.

There were powders and slim shakes and granola bars. She ordered boxes and boxes of cookies with one-fourth the calories of ordinary cookies. What the advertisement didn't tell her is that the cookies were one-fourth the size of ordinary cookies!

And there were the fasts. We never knew if her fasts were for her soul or her body. With Mom's fasts, three, four, five or seven days were scarcely the beginning. Once there was a horrible ten day fast. We lived in dread of her abstinences from food. There were no glazes or braises or pastries.

One year she took a notion that she needed to lose forty pounds before a ladies' retreat in Lufkin, Texas. She rapped up her ambition in a singsong monotony that went like this:

> Made a New Year's resolution
> The first day of the year
> Somethin' I been plannin'
> Since the last time I was here:
> To go on a diet . . . lose forty pounds
> Time I return . . . to the old campgrounds

> To be thin like Sandra Myer
> And trim like Sister Pate
> With a figure like a beanpole
> I simply couldn't wait!
> To go on a diet . . . lose forty pounds
> Time I return . . . to the old campgrounds

> I glanced in the full-length mirror
> Quailed at my reflection

Weighed . . . and Found Wanting

Stepped on the scales–closed my eyes
And looked in the other direction
To go on a diet . . . lose forty pounds
Time I return . . . to the old campgrounds

Bought a case of Nutri-System
The first plan on my docket
But at the end of the month, all I'd lost
Was money from my pocket
Goin' on a diet . . . to lose forty pounds
Time I return . . . to the old campgrounds

Thought I'd try Pat Walkers
Or maybe Figure World
But I couldn't face those leotards
Even in front of the girls
While on a diet . . . to lose forty pounds
Time I return . . . to the old campgrounds

Started counting fat grams on my plate
Carrots, celery, don't eat late
I lost two pounds in the next trimester
Got a box of Aydes as food arrester
Just for my diet . . . to lose forty pounds
Time I return . . . to the old campgrounds

It was April now, half the time was gone
Still looked like a blimp with a towsack on
Gotta get down to business, fast a few days
Cut the chocolate and mend my ways!
'Cause I'm on a diet . . . to lose forty pounds

Mom, I'm Telling On You!

Time I return . . . to the old campgrounds

Then I went jogging for forty-nine miles
Dreaming of dresses in skinny styles
Did chin-ups, push-ups, sit-ups, too
Had gained three pounds when I got through
With my little diet . . . to lose forty pounds
Time I return . . . to the old campgrounds

Time's running out, haven't got much longer
My will is weak, my appetite stronger
Visions of size eights getting dim
With vanishing hopes of being slim
Gotta stick to my diet . . . to lose forty pounds
Time I return . . . to the old campgrounds

Encouraged myself with a nice little saying,
"It's not the winnin', but it's all in the playin'."
Stepped on the scales, and what do you suppose?
Two hundred and ten, not counting my clothes!
Where is that diet . . . to lose forty pounds
Time I return . . . to the old campgrounds?

I've gained ten pounds since resolution day
But you're all my friends, and you love me this way
Bought a size forty . . . and came anyhow
To the Ladies' Retreat . . . at the old campgrounds.

We finally convinced Mom that we like her just the way
she is, every huggable ounce. We all know that the conserva-
tive weight number on her driver's license is not accurate.

Weighed . . . and Found Wanting

We wouldn't think of buying scales for her birthday. Or Valentine's Day. Or her anniversary. Weight is something we don't ever discuss.

We don't even say, "Now, wait . . . !" We might not get that batch of monkey bread if we did.

Tattletales

Mom's prayer life is surely a legend in Heaven. Years ago before children and grandchildren, Mom committed to praying an hour each day. I know of many people who have made the same promise but only one who actually kept it. I've seen Mom pray when she was sick, while she sewed or cooked, or while Dad drove us from one revival to another. She might not pray an hour straight through, but by the end of the day, she got it in. Maybe that is how she kept her sanity while raising her young'n's.

She kept her commitment at any cost. That alone would have been enough for honorable mention in Heaven's Prayer Warrior Hall of Fame. But that was not the only reason Heaven listened. . . .

Chapter Thirteen

Ooze, Ooze— Grab!

Prayer changes things. That is something you should know. Mom changes prayer. That is something you are about to find out.

Prayer meetings were never dull when we prayed beside Mom. She certainly got Heaven's attention every time she prayed if for no other reason than to hear her unusual dialogue. We kids classified her prayers.

There were the happy prayers:

"God, you're just so wonderful I don't hardly know what to do with myself. You, God, are the greatest! I thank You for that hundred dollars I was able to go shopping with yesterday. I know that dress I bought cost thirty dollars, Lord, but it was on sale. Did You see that tag? It had been marked down from ninety-eight dollars to thirty! How much did I save on that, God? Well, You know."

Then there were the serious ones:

"We need to talk." It was time to get down to business when Mom started her prayer like that.

"I need to know if You're going to handle this situation or if You want me to. Now, You know," she would continue, "that if I get a hold of it, I'm not gonna be nice. This has gone on long enough. Now, do You want to deal with it, or shall I?" God surely felt the sincerity of Mom's honest words when she "got serious."

Finally, there were the prayers that were not intended as much for God as for someone nearby to hear. She prayed these prayers to encourage people, to get her point across–and to keep us kids in line.

I will forever remember those famous prayers after I had done an especially terrible deed. Mom would send me to my room (which was next to Mom's and Dad's), and then she would go into her room, throw herself across the bed and begin praying. Loud and long she would wail, begging God to spare her errant children from the wrath that was sure to come. She'd entreat God to give us one more chance, saying she'd rather die and be lost herself than to see us burning in the lake of fire forever and ever. Her prayers would have engaged every smoke and fire detector in the house if we'd had them!

Her honesty in prayer was astonishing. Dad recalls hearing her tell God after His answering a particularly difficult request, "Well, Lord, I didn't think You could do it!"

There was a term used by the older generation called "praying through." Mom believed in praying through. She'd pray through breakfast, lunch, dinner, bedtime and all night long if necessary until she was through the problem at hand. At that point, she would stand and announce that she now had the victory over the problem, and life as we knew it could resume.

You might think that I am making light of Mom's prayers, but you would be wrong. I believed in them and still do. I remember my mother kneeling beside me and praying for our dinner because we were out of food, broke and hungry. We not only had food that day, but we also had dessert and milk and some gas money to go with it all!

One of the more notorious prayers that must have caused giggles in Glory was the prayer we kids called the "ooze, ooze— grab" prayer. Our little church in Temple, Texas, had Tuesday night prayer meetings. These weekly gatherings usually lasted roughly an hour unless someone started praying through. There was no set time limit, but an hour was the norm.

The focus of the meeting one night was the lost souls of our city. Everyone knelt and began praying. Mom made us kids pray by her so that she could keep an eye on our behavior. I and my sisters knelt reverently. After five minutes, kids' prayers are usually over. Mine was, so I started listening to Mom.

"God," she was praying with enthusiastic gusto, "I want Your Spirit to start right here at this bench. Start right here, God. And I want Your Spirit to start oozing down the aisle. Just ooze right down that aisle!" Some people were winding down, but she was just warming up.

"God, just ooze down that aisle, and when You get to the back door, I want Your Spirit to ooze out from under that back door. Just keep oozing, God! Just ooze and ooze across the parking lot, and ooze down the drive and out in the street. And, God, when You get out in that street, I want You to ooze into those cars that are passing by— *And just grab those people and bring them in here!*"

We still talk about the ooze, ooze— grab prayer; it is perhaps the most famous one. But the best ones were those she prayed late at night when she thought we all were asleep.

"Dear God," she'd pray, "I love my kids. I would really like to see them in Heaven. Would You grant that one request for me? I know they're not perfect, and they drive me crazy sometimes. But they are my greatest treasures on earth, and I love them so much it hurts. Help them to see that I really care for them, and let them love me like I love them. Amen." In the echoes of a dark hallway, I would bow my head with tears in my eyes as my heart overflowed with love, and I would repeat the word with her . . . "Amen."

Tattletales

Mom's travels have been a constant source of family entertainment. As her talents in writing and speaking grew, so did the unusual happenings surrounding this ministry. Mom began writing before I was born and has used the medium of journalism and speech to impact countless lives.

She remains to this day one of the most sought after speakers and writers in the south, addressing many denominations and groups of people. This chapter gives a little insight to her special ministry and the fun, fables and foibles that make LaJoyce Martin a legend to her children.

Chapter Fourteen

Going, Going . . . Still Going!

Dad was always a hard worker. He'd get up at a quarter till breakfast and not get back until supper-thirty to complete a job. Mom was a hard worker, too; she just kept a schedule different from Dad's. She'd get up at the crack of noon and work until half past the moon. Mom was a night owl. She loved working at night. She got most of her best stories and inspirations after midnight.

Mom's writing started out as short stories and "*ises*". Here is a sample of one of her *ises*, probably thought up in the wee hours of the morning.

Romance is . . .

> . . . the something made of sweet nothings
> . . . the something in unspoken looks that says more than spoken words
> . . . the something that adds a little heaven to our little time on earth
> . . . the something that makes a loser feel like a winner

   ... the something lovely found in unlikely places: in delivery rooms, on battlefields, behind prison walls, in retirement institutions

   ... the something that fills the emptiest day full of anticipation

   ... the something that is as mortal as today, yet as immortal as tomorrow

   ... the something that enriches the poorest, but without which the richest *are* the poorest

   ... the something, kindled with emotion, that strikes fire to the heart but soothes an inflamed spirit

but best of all,

   ... the something that makes even a nobody feel like a somebody!

After the *is*es came short stories by the hordes, most of which were written for a Sunday School paper for children called Junior Footprints. For years I read the tales in those leaflets with fascination. How could she write such an interesting story? I came to know that Mom had a special gift of prose. That gift was nurtured and advanced until she became a full-fledged author.

Several books later, someone asked Mom to speak at a service devoted to ladies. That was when we discovered another of Mom's hidden talents, that of speaking from the heart so that people go away moved and touched by her words. The mastery of speaking with impact was firmly in her grasp after only a few engagements, and she became sought after for all sorts of events, services and conventions, which bring us to Mom's travels and the stories that naturally follow.

Mom flies to many of her engagements, alleviating the

need to give or understand directions, which is just as well because, for all she is, Mom definitely is not a good navigator! Once she and my aunt, JoAnn Berry, went to Kansas to a retreat where Mom was scheduled to speak. Upon starting home, Aunt JoAnn asked Mom which way to go. (The trip was a rather lengthy one for automobile transportation.)

"Oh, just follow this road," Mom replied with her usual disregard for maps and highways. Sometime later Mom awakened to JoAnn's frantic statement that they were nearly out of gas. Finally asking for directions, they learned that they were on the wrong highway. They had, in fact, not only been on the wrong road for quite some time, but they were also in the wrong state and, according to all indications, were headed directly for the North Pole!

With Mom behind the wheel, any trip becomes a quest for survival. The problem is that she can't talk without the use of her hands. This is okay under normal circumstances, but when she is driving, it creates a dangerous dilemma. One only hopes that she stays on subjects involving straight lines; she could get a ticket for DWI if describing a lava lamp while driving!

Mom loves to fly commercially. She uses the time while flying or driving to write books, and when I say "write," I mean exactly that. Most authors use computers and laptops, but Mom doesn't! She uses a spiral notebook and a pencil.

You see, Mom is not an electric fan. By this I mean that Mom doesn't like electrical gadgets very much. She still uses a hand-operated, metal can opener, and her typewriter is an old Royal manual with a lever that she flings back and forth and a cow bell inside. Nor does she use an electric alarm clock. She still has an old spring driven Mickey Mouse type clock "just in case the electricity goes out."

She writes each new book on a spiral pad or notebook and then ships them to my sister for "computerizing." She says that computers are too difficult to learn, and she doesn't like mice (including the computer mouse and mousepad) anyway.

After many speaking engagements and trips, Mom has learned what to take and what not to take on a trip. Several things are a necessity, like extra pencils, her Dollar Store reading glasses and Kleenex.

On one trip to Tennessee, Mom forgot the Kleenex. It so happened that the speech she gave was a tear-jerker. Everyone, including Mom, was crying and sniffling. Mom reached for her Kleenex, but lo, none could be found! Urgently, she looked for something, anything to use to absorb the moisture. Suddenly she saw it. Just underneath the podium, on a top shelf lay the answer.

In front of hundreds of tear-filled eyes, Mom reached into the pulpit and pulled out a roll of toilet paper. As the audience gawked, she placed the roll on her finger and with her other hand pulled off a long streamer of Charmin and blew her nose! Needless to say, any conviction in the room immediately evaporated, replaced by gales of laughter.

Mom's frantic antics have come to be known far and wide. Being in her company is hilarious, for one never knows what she will say or do next. Sometimes she speaks "off the cuff," saying whatever comes to mind. Now and then her impromptu speeches incorporate some mindless blunders.

In a recent speech, Mom began talking about a particular ailment she had endured. "At one point," she confided to the audience, "we went to see a doctor who gave papaya implants." Mom paused for effect, and the audience sat motionless. *What is a papaya implant?* they wondered. *What part of the body is that?* What she had meant to say was that she had wanted to get an injection of papaya extract. However, the moment was firmly implanted in the minds of the audience forever.

Through all of the travels, meetings and engagements, Mom has remained a steadfast influence in our family, giving comfort and care and praying an hour a day even today. Anyone rich or poor, famous or unknown, no matter his status or station, can relate to Mom and she to him. Famous or infamous, Mom is and will always be, first and foremost, Mother to us kids.

Tattletales

For a couple who never had a date, Mom and Dad made a striking match. God, they will tell you, put them together.

The holy glue held, and that bond has lasted through four decades. From the first strand of romance to the most recent gray hair, this chapter tells all.

Well, almost . . .

Chapter Fifteen

Show and Tell

"Greeings in the Name of Jesus Christ, our Lord and Savior, and soon coming King . . ." I stifled a giggle as I read. Who in the world would ever begin a letter like that? Peeking out to make sure Mother wasn't around, I continued reading. "May the peace of our Lord be with you. . . ." Oh, more and more! It sounded more like Paul's prison epistles than a love letter from Dad to Mother. Anxiously I read, looking for the really mushy stuff.

". . . trust that your family is well. I hope to see you soon but am now with you in spirit. . . ." If this was a love letter, Dad had some serious inhibitions! I was busy scanning the pages when I heard Mom's call to supper. Stuffing the letter into the pile with the others, I quickly closed the aged, tattered relic of a suitcase that held Mom's priceless communiques from years gone by and hurried down the attic stairs to supper.

I could barely constrain myself as I ate. Mom didn't know that I had discovered the old case, and I was determined that she not find out until I had read every letter. There *had* to be some mushy stuff in that faded heap of composition!

After supper, I ran back up the attic steps and turned on

the light. Eagerly I dipped into the valise, picking an envelope at random. "To my Flowersy Girl," it read. *What is a flowersy girl?* I thought as I opened the flap. Extracting a large, cream colored card, I opened it to read the syrupy phrases. Inside was a single line of writing. It said, "To my Darling, thanks for the years together." It was signed by my dad.

Disappointed, I picked up yet another letter. This one was more interesting. Apparently, Dad had been worried about Mom's undying devotion before they married. He had ended his missive: "If you are with me, you are with me. And if you are not, you just are not!" *Duh!* I thought. *That's pretty obvious.*

Impatiently, I grabbed another parcel. This card said, "Thank you for showing me how much you love me!" The words "showing me" had been underlined several lines. I scanned through several more letters with no luck. It seemed that my parents weren't as romantic as I'd presumed.

Bored and distracted, I stood to leave when a folded sheet of yellowed parchment caught my young eyes. Bending down to retrieve it, I planned to place it with the others in the worn carry-all. As I lifted the pages, a small, dried rose fell from its folds. Holding the brittle bud in one hand and the letter in the other, I began to read. It was a poem or maybe a song. It went like this:

I can't sing a love song
Without your harmony.
I can't make it solo;
I need you here with me.
Please, don't leave me lonely,
For, darling, can't you see?

I can't sing a love song
Without your harmony.

So they do love each other, I thought, relieved. With great care I replaced the fragile flower into Mom's journal and left the attic to go on with my life.

But Mom's love letters were not forgotten. We children often had a good laugh about Dad's starchy greetings and his laying down the law to make sure Mother was "with him." For years I watched as Mom and Dad went quietly about their lives, always steady and committed to each other, devoted to their marriage vows. Other couples fell apart under stress; even some of my closest friends fell victim to divorce. Mom and Dad seemed to be unconcerned with the rising divorce rate. Indeed, it was never discussed at all.

How do they do it? I pondered. *They never talk about it, and yet they have this great, steady relationship. How can that be without more expressions of their love from time to time?* (Later I found out that they were plenty expressive but not in front of us kids.) During the initial stages of this book, I found the answers to questions I'd had since childhood.

Mom and Dad celebrated their fortieth anniversary with their family in Morris, Oklahoma, where Dad is serving as pastor. I and the sisters (mostly the sisters) had decorated and prepared for the great celebration. Guests were invited; friends and relatives were there.

We three children were slated to sing several selections, one of which was the song I had found in the attic. As it turned out, the old ballad was a favorite of the celebrated duo during their younger years. As the song wound into the first chorus, I saw Mom silently reach over to take Dad's hand. They sat listening as together we went down memory lane in song. Afterward, there was much cheering and clapping, and someone in the audience yelled, "Speech, speech!" Dad didn't say a word at first; he simply leaned over and kissed Mom.

Amidst the renewed applause, I heard the comment, "Well, I guess that about says it all." Suddenly I had the answers to those questions of long ago. I remembered the words I'd read in the dusty attic amidst the stiff and starchy love letters, ". . . thank you for showing me . . . ." For the first time, I understood that Dad and Mom preferred action over words. Their lives had been spent not just talking about love but actually living it. I watched them holding hands and smiling and knew in that moment that I have two very special parents.

In due course, Mom arose to give a little speech, saying how handsome Dad had become in the last year or so. Enlightened by my new discovery, I watched them closely. As Mom spoke, Dad's eyes turned toward her. He smiled, shaking his head as if she were merely joking.

"No, I mean it," Mom pressed. "He's much better looking now than when we first married." Dad pretended he didn't hear her, but I know he did because the last time I saw them, Mom was wearing a brand-new pair of glasses.

Tattletales

Being the wife of a minister is not always easy. Women often look at the esteemed position with envy, but few actually see the stress and chaos that go along with such an elevated post. Here is a colorful look at Mom, cramming for the preacher's wife exam, and some of the funnier moments that accompanied her tests.

Chapter Sixteen

Going the Extra Smile

"Now, now! They didn't mean all those horrid things they said. They were just upset. You can't act like this!"

"I can't help it!"

"And the Bible says not to call anyone a liar."

"I didn't say they were liars. I just said that their truth has stretch marks all over it!"

"Now, honey . . ."

"I mean it. If they have any truth at all, it's on back order!" It wasn't Mom or Dad who was upset; it was me. I was young, I was mad, and I wasn't the pastor or the pastor's wife. So I could mouth off if I wanted to.

Our church was like many others. We had several new converts full of bright ideas, a passel of old fogeys who said it couldn't be done, and a pastor and pastor's wife who went ahead and did it. Mom and Dad served the call of the ministry without complaint. The stresses of pastoring were many and as densely packed as a can of sardines. Dad could preach out his frustration, I could yell mine out, but Mom— Well, she had to be a little more indirect with hers.

Being a preacher's wife requires patience and restraint,

seasoned liberally with tact. Mom had tact, but she had to work on the patience and restraint. Often we kids were unwitting pawns in her strategic ploys to gain the upper hand in a situation.

One bane of the pastor's house is visitors who cannot tell time. Often people would forget that the clock existed when tarrying at our home, keeping us awake until the wee hours of the morning. My grandfather (I won't say which one) has a sure-fire cure for night owls. When he's had enough fellowship, he stands and announces to the air in general, "Well, let's pray so these good folks can leave. I'm sure they're tired and need to go, so let's let 'em!" Works every time!

But we couldn't get Mom to employ that tactic. She felt she needed to be a little more discreet, so after visiting hours were over, Mom would begin the Bedtime Drama, Act One, Scene One. She'd call us kids into the room where everyone was gathered and then say, "All right. It's getting late now. You kids run along to bed, y'hear me?" She'd say this two or three times very loudly, always asking sweetly if we heard her. We did, and the company did also. Usually that subtle hint was enough to clear the house and enable us all to sleep.

Some of our company, though, seemed to be a mite hard of hearing, whereupon Mother would begin Act One, Scene Two. Since all company meandered into the kitchen before leaving or moving in with us, Mom invented the Cabinet Door Torture. She would open and close cabinet doors noisily, banging pots and pans as sound reinforcement.

"Oh, don't mind me," she would inform our hearing impaired colleagues. "I'm just getting some things done so I can rest tonight." Since one couldn't very well carry on a conversation over the racket, the company either had to sit through the Cabinet Door Torture or go home. Most of the time, our company elected the latter.

There were times when wonderful people would invite us to their house for supper. Mom, being the ever saintly preacher's wife, would never tell the hostess that we didn't like carrot pudding or lasagna made with squash. Rules of etiquette demand that a guest appear pleased with whatever is on the plate. So we learned to hide the burnt squash and ricotta cheese concoction under a large leaf of lettuce and to spread the carrot pudding around so it looked shorter than when first served.

Mom could hold her peace through the worst of meals, but not I. On a particular occasion, the meal tasted like pasteboard cooked in motor oil. The hostess asked if I liked the meal.

"Oh, yes!" I replied without thought.

"Really?" the hostess queried with a smile.

"Sure," I plowed on valiantly. "I like coming here 'cause when we get done, Daddy always takes us to McDonalds for some real food!" I don't remember ever going to that house again.

Then there were saints who brought meals to our house, offering their grandmother's "pickled pork mincemeat casserole" for our dinner. Mom invariably had something nice to say about each dish, no matter how rank it tasted.

"Oh, that pork casserole!" she'd gush. "It was really something else. And so filling. Why just a little bit of that, and I was full!" Interpreted, that meant, "Whatever that awful recipe was, just one bite made me lose my appetite!"

Food wasn't the only thing she endured with grace and dignity. There was a little, old man who played the guitar in our church. He had a bad heart, wore long, skinny ties (I thought they were jumper cables for his pacemaker) and was hard of hearing. He would turn his ancient, tube type amplifier toward Mom and me and then would reach down to turn the volume knob all the way up. Mom would smile and play another chorus while I sat figuring ways to use his guitar for a trot line weight. I admit to being guilty of drastically reducing the intensity of his monotone twanging by moving the knob with my drumstick when he wasn't looking.

Every service he would request that Mom play "In the City Where the Lamb Is the Light." Finally, I got mad and told him we'd play "In the City . . ." as soon as we got there. It seemed to satisfy him; he never asked again.

New converts were Mom's soft spot. She would invite them to the house for a meal and some fellowship. I only remember one exception to the rule. A new member who had just prayed through must have harbored an abundance of Godly love in her heart. To show it, she would hug Dad every time she saw him. Although I'm sure her zeal was entirely innocent, she never was invited to supper. I guess Mom decided she gleaned enough fellowship at church.

One lonely babe in Christ felt the need to come over at least four days a week to ask Mom to "bind together with her in prayer." The dear soul would agonize over everything she could think of, and when she ran out of subjects for intercession, she would start making up things. One day she ran dry of things for which to supplicate. Looking around earnestly, she dropped to her knees in our living room and grabbed two handsful of shag carpet. "God," she beseeched, "make me just like this wall to wall carpet. Right now, God, I want to be like this shag stuff!" I never did know what she meant, but maybe God did.

But the real test of Mother's sainthood came not from errant saints or laggard visitors. It came from her own children. Preachers' kids are not dumb; they're just different. Everything we as PKs did revolved around church. We lived church. For years I thought the refrigerator was invented so we'd have a place to hang our Sunday School art. We had church for breakfast, church for lunch and church for supper, and we got tired of it. It was up to Mom and Dad to keep us interested and to help God keep us saved.

I think the final question on Mom's exam was about me. It was definitely a multiple choice. Someone in the church had said some rather harsh things to me, and I was furious. I wanted justice! They said I had committed some terrible act, and I hadn't even thought of doing it (not that I was always innocent by any means). This time I wanted to get a little of my own revenge.

"But, Mom," I argued, "they couldn't tell the truth standing on the Bible looking at God! It wasn't me. It was that other shrimp next to me!"

"Son, let me tell you something," Mom pulled me into her lap, big as I was, and began talking. In her own tactful way, she told me a story that I will share with you to the best of my faulty memory.

Once there was a young boy at school who was very weak and thin. His family was so poor that he had little to eat. There was another boy in the same class who was rich and had lots of food. Each day the two boys would bring their lunches, the poor one eating peanut butter and crackers while the rich youth munched on savory sandwiches and golden, ripe bananas.

One day the poor boy stole the rich boy's lunch and ate

133

it. As class resumed, the rich youth stood and accused the poor, young stripling, and the teacher called the thief forward.

"You must pay for your crime," the schoolmaster said. "The price is twenty lashes of the whip. Take off your shirt." The quaking schoolboy slowly removed his shirt to reveal nothing but skin and bones. So frail was he that it looked as if the whip should cut him in two. The teacher was moved with compassion but knew that he must administer the penalty. He rolled up his sleeves and raised the whip in preparation for the first, cruel blow.

"Wait!" A great hulk of a boy on the back row sprang forward. "Stop! You can't whip him. It might kill him!"

"Punishment must be served for the crime," the teacher protested. The brawny student paused for only a second and then spoke with determination. "I will take his whipping for him." And so saying, he tore off his shirt and bent over the desk. As lashes were laid on, the strong one flinched and shuddered but never cried out.

Putting on his shirt, he turned to go back to his seat only to find his way blocked by the frail, trembling thief.

"Oh, thank you," the youngster cried, falling at his feet. "Thank you! You took my whipping for me!"

Looking back, I realize that Mom took many, many "whippings" as a minister's wife and as a mother, enduring hardships that were not fair for the sake of sparing another the pain of experience. For myself and for all those lives you spared with your love and selflessness . . . *thank you!*

Tattletales

As a mother, LaJoyce Martin has been through many ordeals while raising her brood. Certainly we as kids have not always been the ideal children to rear, but her love and loyalty have never faltered even in the toughest of times. The following story is my Mother's Day tribute to an awesome Mom . . . who was just a little different.

Chapter Seventeen

My Mom Was Different

My mom just had to be different! Other moms were calm, petite, soft-spoken, easygoing, tame, sane. My mom was six-foot-four, outspoken, straightforward, determined, and almost always right. She was judge, jury and executioner all rolled into one frame.

As the wife of a traveling evangelist, she left skid marks across Texas with her accordion, bent pianos into the shape of bananas and swallowed microphones when she sang.

Yeah, my mom was different in every way. At home, at church, when she drove or when she told Daddy how to drive. She would plop onto the piano bench on Sunday morning and play "Power in the Blood" at full volume when all everyone wanted was "Peace, Peace, Wonderful Peace." She played "Amazing Grace" to the tempo of "I'll Fly Away", and "I'll Fly Away" flew away.

Yeah, my mom was different even when she cleaned the house. If there was something stuck to the carpet while she was vacuuming, she would turn off the old Kirby upright, get down on her hands and knees and pull and scrub until she loosened it. Instead of then putting it into the trash can beside her, she would throw it down and give that old vacuum one more chance!

Yeah, my mom was different even in a crowd. Once we went to a national conference in Anaheim, California. Mom and I took a ride on the elevator together. There are certain formalities that normal people observe in a elevator. Most moms would find a place along the wall, quietly ask the person closest to the buttons to punch "number two, please," and look down at the floor in accordance with elevator rules throughout America.

Not my mom! She stood just inside the door, holding up her leaning hairdo with one hand, and faced the whole crowd, saying in her best southern drawl, "Howdy, y'all!" Most of the people exited at the next floor.

Yeah, my mom was different. She wouldn't let me go to the places other young people in town went, and when I asked her why, she told me, "It's because I love you, my son."

"But, Mom," I would plead, "everybody is doing it!"

"Not everybody," she'd assure me. "You aren't." She got that one right.

I left home and went to college. Then I returned to Texas and married the lovely woman who is now my wife and a lovely mother to our two beautiful daughters. We started out in the world on our own. Along the way, we got hurt and hurt again. I remember calling my mom and dad and taking out my frustrations on them, blaming them for my lot in life as if it was their fault and not my own choice. Most moms would have yelled or argued or hung up but not my mom. She just had to be different. She would hang up and fall on her knees, praying for strength and wisdom both for herself and for her scared and confused son.

Time passed, and one day I and my family lost every one

of our possessions. Most moms would have showered their sons with advice mingled with a few "I told you so"'s. Not my mom, for she was different. She simply said, "Son, God and I are here whenever you need us, whatever you need. You can always talk to both of us–at any time."

I realized then that my mom is special and that although I have made mistakes, her love remains the same. So I called her to apologize for all the things I'd done or not done, said or not said, been or not been. She could have agreed with me, could have been unforgiving or calloused. But my mom was different. She never reminded me of my past, the mistakes, the hurt, the sleepless nights spent in prayer. She didn't talk about the times she spent crying in agony, entreating God's forgiveness when her son had blundered or transgressed. No, my mom simply said three beautiful words, "I forgive you." Then she said three more wonderful, magnificent, healing words, "I love you."

My mom was different. She surely was. And because she was different . . . she made a difference in me.